Idi Amin

Other books in the Heroes and Villains series include:

Heroes and Villains

Idi Amin

James Barter

LUCENT BOOKS
An imprint of Thomson Gale, a part of The Thomson Corporation

THOMSON
™
GALE

...roit • New York • San Francisco • San Diego • New Haven, Conn. • Waterville, Maine • London • Munich

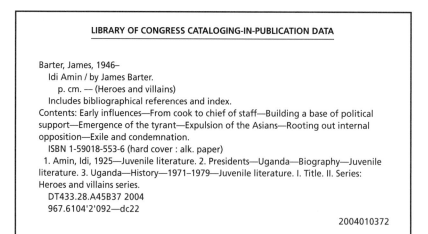

THOMSON
™
GALE

For more information, contact
Lucent Books
27500 Drake Rd.
Farmington Hills, MI 48331-3535
Or you can visit our Internet site at http://www.gale.com

LIBRARY OF CONGRESS CATALOGING-IN-PUBLICATION DATA

Barter, James, 1946–
    Idi Amin / by James Barter.
        p. cm. — (Heroes and villains)
    Includes bibliographical references and index.
Contents: Early influences—From cook to chief of staff—Building a base of political
support—Emergence of the tyrant—Expulsion of the Asians—Rooting out internal
opposition—Exile and condemnation.
    ISBN 1-59018-553-6 (hard cover : alk. paper)
    1. Amin, Idi, 1925—Juvenile literature. 2. Presidents—Uganda—Biography—Juvenile
literature. 3. Uganda—History—1971–1979—Juvenile literature. I. Title. II. Series:
Heroes and villains series.
    DT433.28.A45B37 2004
    967.6104'2'092—dc22
                                                                2004010372

Printed in the United States of America

Contents

Good and evil are an ever-present feature of human history. Their presence is reflected through the ages in tales of great heroism and extraordinary villainy. Such tales provide insight into human nature, whether they involve two people or two thousand, for the essence of heroism and villainy is found in deeds rather than in numbers. It is the deeds that pique our interest and lead us to wonder what prompts a man or woman to perform such acts.

Samuel Johnson, the eminent eighteenth-century English writer, once wrote, "The two great movers of the human mind are the desire for good, and fear of evil." The pairing of desire and fear, possibly two of the strongest human emotions, helps explain the intense fascination people have with all things good and evil—and by extension, heroic and villainous.

People are attracted to the person who reaches into a raging river to pull a child from what could have been a watery grave for both, and to the person who risks his or her own life to shepherd hundreds of desperate black slaves to safety on the Underground Railroad. We wonder what qualities these heroes possess that enable them to act against self-interest, and even their own survival. We also wonder if, under similar circumstances, we would behave as they do.

Evil, on the other hand, horrifies as well as intrigues us. Few people can look upon the drifter who mutilates and kills a neighbor or the dictator who presides over the torture and murder of thousands of his own citizens without feeling a sense of revulsion. And yet, as Joseph Conrad writes, we experience "the fascination of the abomination." How else to explain the overwhelming success of a book such as Truman Capote's *In Cold Blood*, which examines in horrifying detail a vicious and senseless murder that took place in the American heartland in the 1960s? The popularity of murder mysteries and Court TV are also evidence of the human fascination with villainy.

Most people recoil in the face of such evil. Yet most feel a deep-seated curiosity about the kind of person who could commit a terrible act. It is perhaps a reflection of our innermost fears that we wonder whether we could resist or stand up to such behavior in our presence or even if we ourselves possess the capacity to commit such terrible crimes.

The Lucent Books Heroes and Villains series capitalizes on our fascination with the perpetrators of both good and evil by introducing readers to some of history's most revered heroes and hated villains. These include heroes such as Frederick Douglass, who knew firsthand the humiliation of slavery and, at great risk to himself, publicly fought to abolish the institution of slavery in America. It also includes villains such as Adolf Hitler, who is remembered both for the devastation of Europe and for the murder of 6 million Jews and thousands of Gypsies, Slavs, and others whom Hitler deemed unworthy of life.

Each book in the Heroes and Villains series examines the life story of a hero or villain from history. Generous use of primary and secondary source quotations gives readers eyewitness views of the life and times of each individual as well as enlivens the narrative. Notes and annotated bibliographies provide stepping-stones to further research.

ONE FROG SPOILS A WATERHOLE

Idi Amin, who preferred to be called "Big Daddy," will go down in history as one of the most vilified mass murderers of the twentieth century. Self-proclaimed president of Uganda, Amin illegally seized power in a military coup in 1971 and tyrannically ruled 10 million fellow Ugandans until he fled the African country in 1979. In his wake, Amin left deplorable examples of brutality, torture, murder, and demented personal behavior. During his eight years of barbaric rule, an estimated three hundred thousand Ugandans were killed by his orders.

Referred to by many world leaders and historians as the "Hitler of Africa" —a reference to the genocidal German dictator whom Amin once admitted admiring—Amin became known for his psychopathic cruelty. For many of the three hundred thousand who died from his human rights abuses, death was welcome relief following well-documented tortures such as beatings, rape, and dismemberment.

Amin's penchant for inappropriate clownlike antics followed by bizarre and sadistic behavior revealed a severe psychological imbalance. A capricious tyrant, he was capable of displaying silly behavior one moment and horrifying, grotesque behavior the next. Amin once bemused heads of state in a 1978 meeting by publicly proclaiming himself, "His Excellency President for Life, Field Marshal Al Hadji Doctor Idi Amin, Lord of All the Beasts of the Earth and Fishes of the Sea, and Conqueror of the British Empire in Africa in General and Uganda in Particular."[1] Such examples of juvenile behavior gave him a reputation as a buffoon who was quietly laughed at by other government leaders. On the other hand, he was also known to brag about practicing cannibalism, feeding people to crocodiles, and storing his enemies' heads in a refrigerator at his beach house, although these claims have not been confirmed.

During Amin's tyranny, no coherent political policies were ever enacted. Amin failed to implement a foreign or domestic policy and failed to institute any social services or economic strategies to benefit his people. Due to Amin's reckless statesmanship and lack of understanding of complex economic forces, Uganda's economy collapsed, trapping millions in poverty far worse than they had suffered under the leadership of Milton Obote, the man he overthrew.

One man who knew Amin well, Dr. Sunny Orumen Akhigbe, said shortly after Amin's death in 2003 while exiled in Saudi Arabia: "He was simply a beast. Now, he is gone, dragging his memory down the wrong lane of history. Imagine a former head of state, buried in an unmarked grave, having no single monument to his name in his country, Uganda."[2] Newspaper headlines announcing Amin's death were even less kind than Dr. Akhigbe. The *London Times* headline proclaimed, "Idi Amin the Butcher of Uganda Dies Pining for Home," while another London newspaper, the *People*, reported, "Monster Amin Dead—No Tears As Murderous Dictator Idi Amin Dies." The *Manches-ter Guardian* carried a more provocative headline, "Idi Goes to Hell," while the *New York Times* ran, "Idi Amin, Murderous and Erratic Ruler of Uganda in the 70's, Dies in Exile."

Two men once close to Amin provide two points of view, both of which

Idi Amin ruled Uganda from 1971 to 1979, leaving brutality, torture, murder, and demented behavior as a legacy.

highlight Amin's split personality. In his book *A State of Blood: The Inside Story of Idi Amin*, Henry Kyemba, once the minister of health under Amin, made this observation about his personality:

> To me, he was always charming and easy to work with, but he also displayed a ruthless and cunning practicality, individuality, and enterprise. For the first time I saw the effects of his particular intelligence which allowed him to snatch any advantage unconsciously offered and turn it to his own advantage.[3]

Dr. Solomon Asea, a physician and former Ugandan ambassador to the United States, presented this diagnosis of Amin's mental capacity: "In a medical sense, I think it is safe to say that he was crazy. He could kill a person one minute and the next he'd be laughing and playing the guitar with no apparent recollection of what he'd done."[4]

Other people have asked how it was possible for Amin to remain in power for eight years without the intervention of other nations that knew the horrors of his regime. One answer, from historians Thomas and Margaret Melady in their book *Idi Amin Dada*, suggests that other countries were afraid: "It was not the nature of African nations to interfere in the affairs of other bordering nations for fear

At an outdoor rally a fully decorated Amin points into the crowd. Clearly insane, Amin was described as "simply a beast."

of later reprisals."[5] However, some countries did not interfere because they approved of Amin and even conducted business with him. Kenneth Ingram, in his book *Obote: A Political Biography*, notes that Amin's despotism was "supported by funding from other dictators. Libya's Muammar Qaddafi bankrolled Amin as did a handful of Middle Eastern Muslim nations suspicious of Israeli and American foreign interests on the African Continent."[6]

On a much larger scale, Amin's reckless behavior destroyed more than innocent Ugandan lives. It also contributed to the destruction of Africa's image around the world. During Amin's eight-year reign, nations outside the African Continent gawked at his barbaric, irrational behavior that reinforced the view of many non-African national leaders that central African countries were primitive.

Amin himself was an acute embarrassment within the African Continent. According to David Gwyn, who lived in Uganda and worked for Amin, "Amin was a living example of the Ugandan proverb, one frog spoils a waterhole."[7] What Gwyn meant by his metaphor is that the poison that Amin spread in Uganda overshadowed all the good done by other African countries.

To this day, Ugandans struggle to regain the international reputation their nation once enjoyed as the "Pearl of Africa," as the British diplomat Sir Winston Churchill once called it in 1907 in his book *My African Journey*. And today, there is still much to be learned about Amin's dictatorship and how he orchestrated his rise to power.

Chapter One

EARLY INFLUENCES

Idi Amin was exposed to many factors as a boy that would later influence his behavior during his authoritarian rule. Some of these influences, such as his parents, his tribal culture, and growing up in a small village, provided Amin with values that remained with him for life. On a larger scope, through experiencing life under British colonial rule and racism practiced by the British against black Ugandans, as well as witnessing long-standing animosities among Ugandan tribes, Amin learned valuable tactics about coercion and manipulation that he would apply as leader of Uganda.

Amin's Early Childhood

Idi was born between 1923 and 1925; although the exact date is still disputed, most historians accept 1925 as the most likely year. He was born into the Kakwa tribe, the tribe of his father, in the village of Koboko in northwest Uganda, close to the borders of the Democratic Republic of Congo to the west and Sudan to the North.

The Kakwa were members of the greater Nubian Nation, a group of tribes originally from the Nubian Desert in Sudan. Idi's Nubian ancestors were originally brought into Uganda as mercenaries for Ugandan warlords. According to historian David Martin: "Among their fellow countrymen, they enjoyed an unenviable reputation for having one of the world's highest homicide rates. The Nubians were renowned for their sadistic brutality, lack of formal education, for poisoning enemies, and for their refusal to integrate, even in the urban centers."[8]

Idi's father was Andreas Nyabire, who was born in 1889 and raised as a Catholic. When he converted to Islam in 1910, he changed his name to Amin Dada. He served in the King's African Rifles (KAR) from 1915 to 1920. This was a corps of African soldiers under the command of the British, who at that time had colonized and controlled much of Central Africa. In 1921 Amin Dada joined the Uganda Police, where his job was to administer corporal punishments called *kibooko* to natives. Such punishments included severe beatings with whips and sticks, cigarette burns, and the breaking of fingers and toes.

Shortly after Idi's birth, his father abandoned the family, not to return until Idi was a grown man. His mother, Assa Aatte, was left to care for young Amin and his older brother and sister. Assa was from a tribe in northeastern Uganda that enjoyed friendly relations with the Kakwa. After Assa's husband departed, she moved the family closer to her small village near the larger city of Jinja. There, she worked on sugarcane plantations owned by wealthy

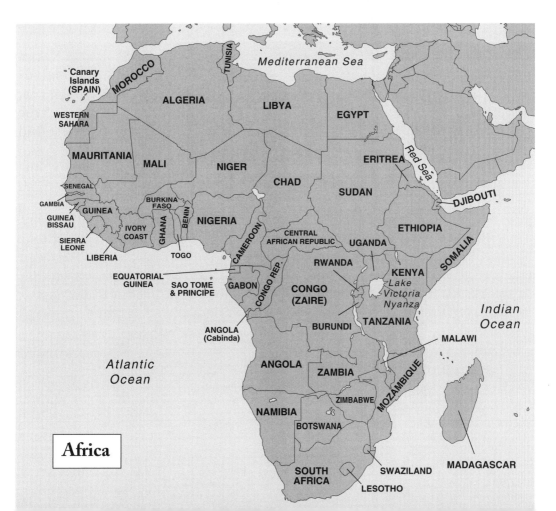

Africa

Asian families who carried on business in Uganda under the protection of the British and the KAR. Ever since the mid-nineteenth century when the British entered Uganda and other central African nations to exploit the countries' natural resources, Asian families were encouraged by the British to manage plantations and other businesses. While Assa worked on the plantations, she and her three children went to live with a Nubian corporal in the KAR, and she worked for other KAR men and their families, cleaning clothes and polishing boots. Assa also earned extra money as a traditional herbalist helping women with fertility complications and pregnancy and as a practitioner of witchcraft. Altogether, her many jobs provided just barely enough money to keep the four of them fed and clothed.

Young Amin attended a missionary school for a short time, dropping out when he completed the fifth grade. It was about that time that both his older brother and sister died. Between 1936 and 1938 Amin and his mother lived with Assa's relatives, where he helped herd goats, carry water from the Nile River for cooking and cleaning, and till the soil to earn money for his family. He then moved to the home of Sheikh

The Effect of British Racism on Young Amin

While growing up, Amin suffered racism that he recounted from time to time as a painful experience for a young boy. Amin carried memories of both his and his mother's exclusions from socializing with the British due to their race. Although Amin was eager to please the British soldiers, whom he admired, he also acquired a hatred for them that would later play out in his political agenda as dictator.

One of the men who knew Amin best and understood the pain that Amin had suffered from racism was Henry Kyemba, one of his ministers. Kyemba comments in his book, *A State of Blood: The Inside Story of Idi Amin*, that Amin "carried the scars of British racism," and that when he was dictator, "Amin was always eager to humiliate whites, especially his former British masters." Kyemba commented in his book that during a ceremony requiring subjects to swear an oath of allegiance normally done standing, Amin demanded they kneel. "To force the whites to kneel was—as he told me—a deliberate insult," writes Kyemba.

Amin desired revenge for his boyhood experiences of British racism. Indeed, much of his quest for Ugandan nationalism and pride as an adult stemmed from his desire to rise above the British.

Idi Amin grew up along the banks of the upper Nile River.

Ahmed Hussein in the town of Semuto, where he spent two years working and learning to recite the Koran, the holy book of Muslims.

Young Amin also spent time fishing on the southern leg of the Nile River not far from its source in Lake Victoria. From Lake Victoria the Nile carved its way north, carrying with it an abundant supply of fish and precious water for crops grown along its banks. In his later years, when talking with friends, Amin spoke of the joys of his fishing days and appreciation for his mother's tribal stretch of the Nile.

During Amin's later teenage years, he divided his time between fishing, sports, and jobs, which ranged from a doorman at the Imperial Hotel in Jinja to selling *mandazis*, a type of donut, on the city streets, to working odd jobs for soldiers. Amin also enjoyed friendships with the older soldiers, preferring their company to that of his teenage friends.

Perhaps his mother's greatest influence on Amin was her practice of witchcraft, considered an honorable profession in central African nations at that time. Amin accompanied her from place to place watching and learning some of her craft. These lessons remained with him all of his life.

Amin and Witchcraft

By the time Amin was sixteen he had adopted many of the supernatural beliefs that are a part of witchcraft. As Assa moved about in search of plantation work or work in KAR barracks, Amin learned from her about the mythology surrounding witchcraft, locally known as *juju/marabou*, and how witchcraft could be used to influence peoples' behavior or affect their health.

Many villagers struggling with medical and personal problems came to Assa. In addition to the use of herbal remedies to help them, she taught Amin how to perform a variety of animal sacrifices. According to the rituals of her *juju/marabou*, this included either the beheading of the animal or the dismemberment of some body parts such as the tongue, nose, ears, eyes, heart, or lips. On occasion, a sacrificial animal was buried alive. Depending upon the nature of the illness or personal problem, Assa might also recommend that the person eat various animal vital organs or drink small amounts of its blood.

In addition to healing the sick and solving personal problems, *juju/marabou* rituals could also be used to curse personal enemies. Under such circumstances, rituals were aimed at causing death or injury to the offending person.

The many rituals of *juju/marabou* played a major role in the lives of most central African people. All respected villagers and tribal leaders either participated in rituals or had a keen understanding of the cultural importance of witchcraft. Some tribal members practiced an exotic mixture of *juju/marabou* and Catholicism, which Idi learned from observation.

Tribal Loyalties

Young Amin quickly learned the unswerving importance of tribal loyalties. When Ugandans were asked who they were or where they were from, they first identified the name of their tribe. Within Amin's Uganda there existed a blend of many different ethnic, religious, and tribal groups. When balancing loyalty to one's tribe and loyalty to Uganda as a national entity, Ugandans almost always favored the tribe. Amin grew up at a time when national goals and policies were rarely known outside of Uganda's capital city of Kampala. If they were known, few rural tribes felt obligated to meet or obey them.

Due to tribal loyalties, which in some cases dated back more than a thousand years, Ugandans trusted neighboring tribes and mistrusted those farther away. When Amin traveled with his mother from her tribal grounds along the Nile in eastern Uganda to the Kakwa tribal grounds of his father, she taught him which roads would be safe and which to avoid for reasons of tribal rivalries.

Tribal tattoos could quickly identify a person's tribe. Traditional tribal tattoos generally depicted some free-form design, animal, or geographical landmark unique to each tribe's territory and history. Young Amin, who claimed two tribal allegiances because his parents

came from different tribes, never acquired a tattoo, but his father had one on
his shoulder indicating he was Kakwa.

As a teenager hanging around military barracks, Amin learned that he
could use his tribal connections to further himself. He observed tribal leaders
achieving personal success by fostering
a willingness to carry out the foreign
policy of the British. Occasional conflict, for example, sometimes broke out
between Asian plantation managers and
Ugandan fieldworkers over pay and
treatment. In most cases, the British
policy was to keep the fieldworkers toil-

ing regardless of their complaints—
sometimes using force to do so. The
British sought Ugandan tribal leaders
willing to impose British policy and rewarded them for their loyalty.

The British carefully selected leaders from the most powerful tribes to
act as stern foremen, keeping the workers moving on the British-owned and
-operated cotton, rubber, and sugarcane
plantations. At the same time, these
leaders fought side-by-side with the
British to repress any tribal opposition
to the British. Amin also noticed that
some Ugandan tribes were favored by

Distinctive hairdos, tattoos, and adornments identify African tribal members.

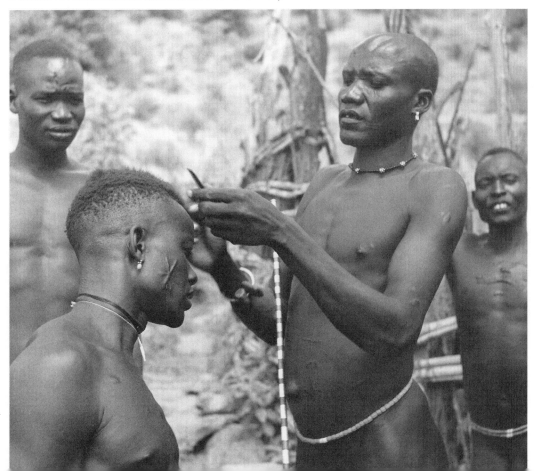

the British over others. Part of British foreign policy was to give financial and material rewards, such as tools, clothing, and simple furniture, to tribes that could be trusted to support British decisions affecting Ugandans. Fortunately for Amin, the Kakwa along with other Nubian tribes were in favor because of their willingness to send young men into the military to support British commercial ventures and to control lawlessness by rival tribes. This keen awareness of how the British successfully controlled the nation by manipulating tribes was valuable to Amin.

Ambivalence Toward the British

As a young man in his late teens, Amin saw the British soldiers as role models. Amin's tribal members described him as eager to please British officers and administrators. He sought to emulate them by dressing in clothes similar to the British, attending military parades along with his friends, copying the marching style of the British troops, and listening

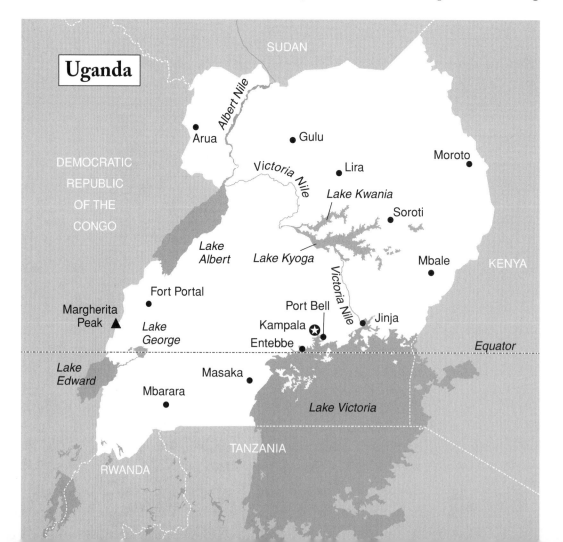

The King's African Rifles, a corps of African soldiers under British command, protected British interests in Africa.

to their bagpipe music. He was known to march his friends around the dusty streets while humming Scottish bagpipe music and to berate them for marching out of step and wearing dirty clothes.

Always on the lookout for new recruits for their army, British officers took notice of Amin. He insisted on carrying the British flag whenever the soldiers invited young Ugandans to join in their parades. Marching at the head of a column, Amin learned just enough English to respond to orders with a crisp "Yes, sir" and "Right you are, sir,"

the only English he learned for years. The officers also noticed that, standing a head taller than most of his friends and blessed with an unusually muscular build, Amin was beginning to develop a powerful physique.

In his later teens, Amin nurtured a love for sports. From watching the British soldiers, he learned to play rugby, a British form of football similar to that played in the United States but much more violent. By this time, standing six feet two and weighing two hundred pounds, he was taller and heavier than

The King's African Rifles

The army that Amin belonged to had its origins in the latter half of the nineteenth century. At that time, several British companies had set up plantations and businesses in Uganda and other African nations. The British government established an army to protect its commercial interests. Named the King's African Rifles (KAR), this army not only protected British interests but also waged war from time to time on behalf of African governments against rebel armies.

For young men such as Amin, who excelled in military activities, the KAR was the only army in Uganda they could join. Since the British controlled the army, Britain was able to control the politics of Uganda. The demand for soldiers in the KAR was great. Amin was encouraged to join the KAR in part because such a force could not possibly be supplied entirely by the British, prompting them to enlist large numbers of trustworthy Ugandans to join the ranks. The distinction, and sometimes point of conflict, for Amin, was that the officers were British and the foot soldiers Ugandan. This division, one of both nationality and race, became an increasingly sore point between the two when Amin became a member. To add an even greater sense of tension between the two nationalities, the Ugandan soldiers requested British citizenship as one form of compensation for their dedication, but their requests were repeatedly denied.

The interests of the British military and African soldiers were quite often contradictory, and it took an ongoing process of negotiation and accommodation of Ugandan soldiers to keep the soldiers fighting and to make the army effective. Amin and a small number of other Ugandans were invited by British officers to join the officers' ranks. Such promotions were offered as a way of keeping the Ugandan troops loyal to British objectives.

most British soldiers and capable of knocking them over when he ran with the ball. Amazed by his strength and speed, the British invited him to practice with their team and struck up casual friendships with him.

In spite of his friendly relations with some of the British troops, Amin realized that he would never be accepted by them as an equal. He was welcome to practice with the rugby team and to hang out with soldiers around the barracks while his mother worked there, but beyond that he was not invited to participate in any of their other activities.

Amin was also aware of and bothered by battles that broke out from time to time between the KAR and Ugandan natives, which sometimes led to the deaths of natives. The KAR intervened in a variety of circumstances such as intertribal conflict, cattle rustling and plantation labor disputes, and tribal insurrections to force the British out of Uganda. Watching the KAR British officers and Ugandan foot soldiers depart from the barracks and listening to the stories they told, Amin learned that the British officers expected the Ugandan troops, not the British officers, to do the actual fighting and killing. This situation was a growing cause of tension and ambivalence in Uganda and for Amin.

Watching his mother work on the sugarcane plantations for pitifully low wages was another problem for Amin. He knew that the British owned and controlled the cotton, sugarcane, tea, and rubber plantations, and sent the products back to Britain while paying native Ugandans little for their labors. Another source of irritation for Amin and Ugandans was racism. The British preferred to hire Asians to run British

This photograph depicts an industrialized Algiers. Colonialists pointed to European-built cities and railroads in Africa as proof of white superiority.

businesses, plantations, and shops because they believed them to be more efficient, smarter, and more trustworthy than Ugandans. The Ugandans felt that the British were exploiting them and that they were treating black Ugandans as inferior to both the Asians and the British. On a personal level, Amin understood his countrymen's bitterness because he had frequently asked to play in regulation rugby games but was always told that he could only play during practices because the games were for whites only.

Amin Confronts Colonial Racism

During the mid-nineteenth century, there existed the commonplace stereotype, found among both whites and blacks, that white Europeans were intellectually superior to black Africans.

European missionaries believed it their moral duty to convert natives to Christianity.

As a way of confirming this notion of superiority, Europeans pointed to the new technologies they were introducing to Africa. Most notable and revolutionary were railroads and steamships, neither of which had been seen there before the colonial period. Europeans also pointed to the establishment of large plantations producing bumper crops, factories manufacturing a variety of useful products, and a system of laws and courts to dispense justice.

Cecil Rhodes, a British entrepreneur who made a fortune mining precious metals in Africa, once commented, "I contend that we are the first race in the world, and that the more of the world we inhabit the better it is for the human race."[9] This attitude had become institutionalized by Amin's time. It was especially evident in the larger cites such as Kampala, where the better residential areas were reserved for British and Asians, who were strictly separated from the local population. Added to this sense of superiority among many Europeans was the belief that they had a moral obligation to convert African populations from their local tribal religions to Christianity. Acting on this belief, the British Anglican and the Roman Catholic churches sent hundreds of missionaries to Africa to live among the tribes and to convert them to Christianity.

Amin also saw evidence of white superiority practiced in the military, where only whites were allowed into the officer ranks, leaving the most undesirable jobs to local black troops. He was also aware that Assa had tried to enroll him in schools but was turned down because the schools established by the British were open only to the children of British businessmen, diplomats, and army officers. Although such policies angered Amin, he joked about it in the presence of the British to mask his anger.

Even though Amin had reasons to dislike the British because of their unfair treatment of Ugandans, he became attracted to the military life they could offer him. They could provide him with a future preferable to that of his peers, who mainly chopped sugarcane in the hot fields or worked on the Nile docks loading heavy bales of cotton onto barges bound for Britain. And besides, the strict military regimen suited his personality.

Chapter Two

From Cook to Chief of Staff

At the age of twenty-one, Amin took his first step toward the pinnacle of Ugandan power. While playing rugby and picking up extra money cleaning and polishing boots at the KAR barracks, Amin caught the eye of a British officer, who noted Amin's energy, enthusiasm, and his willingness to please the officers. Sensing he might be a reliable employee, the officer offered Amin full-time employment working in the barracks as a cook. Although Amin had little education and spoke only a few words of English, the British valued other qualities such as his powerfully built physique and aggressive manner that gave him an edge over his peers.

Not only did Amin have steady employment cooking and cleaning, but he was now a *dupi*, a person with a status slightly elevated above the traditional servile status of most uneducated Ugandans employed by the British. Following a short stint in the kitchen, Amin was inducted into the corps of soldiers because he was big and burly and fit the profile of an ideal foot soldier in the KAR. In fact, Amin's six-foot-four, 230-pound frame stood out among other African fighters. Amin established a reputation as a conscientious soldier who enthusiastically carried out orders. He impressed his commanders with his zeal, and he was alert, responsive to orders, and well polished. He excelled as a marksman and overall he was perceived as a splendid and reliable soldier.

From the standpoint of the KAR leaders, Amin was a natural soldier. One key element for success in the military was the ability to intimidate, and Amin, they reasoned, would do well on jungle patrols as a man who could push his way into village homes searching for weapons.

Those with ties to the Nubian tribes were favored by the officers over other Ugandans and feared by everyone else. Noticing Amin's willingness to take orders and to ferociously punish violators of British law, the British promoted Amin to the rank of corporal in 1948. Shortly thereafter, he further ingratiated himself with British officers by winning the heavyweight boxing championship of the army and then of all of Uganda. Regarding Amin's potential for army promotion when the British were look-

ing to promote Ugandans, known to the British officers as "black chaps," Major Iain Grahame stated the dilemma rather bluntly:

We looked among the ranks of our soldiers and thought: Who the hell are going to be the officers? On recruiting, we always went for the black chaps who were young and strong and ran quicker than anyone else. We had a choice between the loyal long-service chaps, who were absolutely reliable, but incredibly limited by their lack of

The King's African Rifles often suppressed uprisings among fellow countrymen. Amin was considered an ideal candidate for the corps.

Amin the Sportsman

Amin gained early popularity with tribal friends and local British soldiers because he excelled at nearly all types of sports. Amin prided himself as an accomplished sportsman. His muscular build coupled with an attitude of winning at any cost garnered the respect of his countrymen.

Amin's greatest and earliest claim to athleticism was his boxing ability. He held Uganda's heavyweight boxing championship from 1951 to 1960, during some of which time he was also the heavyweight champion of the army. For years Amin had a reputation as a powerful puncher capable of knocking out opponents. He delighted in traveling from town to town fighting any man willing to climb into the ring with him. His strategy was to block his opponent in a corner so he could not escape and then mercilessly pound his body.

Amin participated in other sports as well. Second to boxing he loved to play rugby, where he excelled at running over opponents and from time to time knocking some unconscious. He also liked less violent sports such as tennis and swimming. Wherever he traveled, Amin enjoyed regular exercise in pools. He even took up car racing in 1974 when he participated in the Pan African Road Rally driving a French Citröen.

In a rare interview when Amin was asked what he wanted to be known for when he died, he answered that he would like to be remembered as a great athlete.

In his youth Amin was Uganda's heavyweight boxing champ.

intelligence—Idi was a typical example—or newly recruited chaps with slightly more intelligence but absolutely no experience.[10]

Building a Reputation

Between 1952 and 1954, Amin fought for the British in the Mau Mau Wars, his first foray into battle. The Mau Mau Wars were a series of guerrilla wars fought by rebel tribes in Kenya attempting to expel the British. When violence occurred, leading to the murder of British subjects, the King of England ordered the KAR to take action.

In the course of the war, Amin's flare for brutality, which would later become the hallmark of his rule as president of Uganda, caught the attention of his superiors. Amin distinguished himself by his willingness to attack with unusual fury and to kill without hesitation, often preferring to use his machete to hack his enemies to death than to shoot them with his pistol.

British officers, however, noted something else that both concerned and amazed them. They had experienced little success interrogating rebels about where they had hidden their weapons. Amin stepped forward, volunteering to get the information if he would be allowed to handle it his own way. The British agreed but were shocked at his method. According to historian George Ivan Smith in his book *Ghosts of Kampala: The Rise and Fall of Idi Amin*: "Africans being interrogated by Amin

were made to stand alongside a table. Each was ordered to place his penis on the table surface. Amin stood beside them, machete in hand, asking the question, 'Where are the weapons?' and getting rapid responses."[11]

Amin's reputation as a man to be feared and respected was born. His name appeared on the list of those soldiers who performed best during the Mau Mau Wars. He was nominated for promotion to the new rank of *effendi*, the equivalent of a sergeant and the highest rank attainable by a black man. In 1954 Amin was selected to march in a parade honoring Queen Elizabeth, and later that same year Sergeant Amin led the honor guard to welcome a delegation of visiting ambassadors. Major Iain Grahame, who was Amin's commander, commented on his leadership qualities:

> It was clear even in 1953 that Idi was an outstanding leader. He was brave, showed initiative, fought mercilessly, and was a great athlete. He could not speak any English except to say "good morning, sir" and "yes sir" but it was obvious that he would get promoted fairly rapidly, despite the fact that he was terribly handicapped by his obvious lack of education.[12]

The British officers who saw Amin in action may not have liked or condoned his brutal behavior, yet they were impressed by its effectiveness. Although a few voices warned that Amin needed to be reined in, others saw that he could get results when dealing with Ugandan tribes, and they encouraged his savage battlefield conduct with special privileges and promotions.

Grisly Success

If Sergeant Amin's actions in the Mau Mau Wars were not clear indicators of his true nature, then those of the Turkana uprising left little doubt. In 1962, the Turkana tribesmen were rustling cattle from neighboring tribes and the KAR was called in to stop the thieving. By this time, Uganda was nearing an agreed upon independence from the British, and Ugandan officers were allowed to be promoted above the rank of *effendi*. Amin had risen through the ranks from *effendi* to lieutenant to captain to major. He commanded a group of soldiers that had been ordered to enter the territory and disarm the rustlers. Contrary to his orders, which were to arrest the rustlers and seize their weapons, Amin ordered dozens of suspected cattle rustlers summarily shot and killed and then left unburied to be eaten by hyenas.

Mau Mau rebels sit in a cramped Kenyan prison. Amin's brutal nature showed in his dealing with prisoners.

Amin's Role in the Mau Mau Wars

During the early 1950s, a revolt broke out in Kenya initiated by the Kikuyu, Embu, and Meru tribes over prime agricultural land unfairly taken by the Europeans. Dubbed by the British as the Mau Mau Wars, a term taken from the Mau Mau mountain range on the western side of Kenya, the wars marked a turning point in the struggle for independence of Africans from a century of British colonial domination.

The British responded to the revolt by dispatching several divisions of the KAR, one of which included Amin's "E" unit, to quell the war. Amin built his reputation as a ferocious fighter between 1952 and 1954. In 1952 he distinguished himself as a young warrior during his first foray into battle when he killed for the first time. At that battle, which occurred in a dense forest occupied by the Kikuyu, Amin lead a squad of foot soldiers behind enemy lines and was able to sneak up and annihilate their entire contingent.

Amin won fame for his ability to fight without using modern weapons. His commanders were impressed by his ability to kill without guns because he could do so silently. Amin's boyhood experiences of hunting and trapping animals along the Nile had taught him to effectively use vines to choke the enemy from behind, and to dig pit traps into which enemy soldiers fell and were then easily killed.

This grisly solution to the cattle rustlers was just the beginning of a long string of brutalities. In a related incident, Amin lost his patience while interrogating Turkana tribesmen about rustlers. Because he was not getting the information he wanted, he ordered their castration, one by one, until someone was willing to talk. After eight suspects had been castrated, he got the information he needed.

In another example of Amin's penchant for violence, while pursuing a group of cattle rustlers, Amin's platoon gathered together a group of villagers and interrogated them about the whereabouts of suspected thieves. Receiving little useful information, Amin ordered a variety of tortures until they talked. In an apparent attempt to establish a reputation as a brutal officer, Amin then executed twelve of the torture victims by laying them on their backs, crushing their chests with his rifle butt, and stomping on them with his feet. He then ordered their relatives to dig their graves and bury them.

The British heard about the brutal murders and were furious. The commander of the KAR, Sir Walter Coutts, expressed the need for a court-martial. British KAR officers might be stern when dealing with thieving tribal members, but they would not tolerate unchecked brutality. To the British, acts of viciousness toward innocent villagers such as those displayed by Amin only served to anger them. Although Coutts recommended a court-martial hearing, he decided to defer the decision because, at that time, Uganda was in the process of gaining its independence from Britain. He knew that in a few months the first Ugandan prime minister, Dr. Milton Obote, would take office and Coutts decided to let him deal with Amin rather than interfere with an internal Ugandan problem.

Obote, who had not yet met Amin but knew that he was one of only two black Ugandan officers in the KAR, wished to promote blacks, not remove them. For that reason Obote decided to do nothing more than reprimand him. Coutts, gravely disappointed in what he perceived to be Obote's lack of insight in this matter, responded, "I warn you this officer could cause you trouble in the future."[13] In spite of Coutts's warnings about Amin, Obote insisted that he would take no punitive action against him. Later Obote wrote, "I regret to say that part of Uganda's present suffering, sickness, and inhumanity can be traced to the opinion I gave to Sir Walter."[14]

Although Obote had been warned about potential future troubles with Amin, he gradually brought Amin closer to the inner circle of Ugandan authority. As time went on and as Obote struggled to maintain authority in the face of growing opposition, he found value in keeping Amin close to him.

Ugandan Independence

On October 9, 1962, Ugandans celebrated their independence from Britain. Without this historic handover of authority, Amin would most likely have passed his entire life uneventfully in the KAR. But on the eve of independence from the British, Uganda's future looked bright. While the neighboring countries of Kenya and Tanzania resorted to bloody insurrections to secure their freedom, Uganda watched as the British withdrew, leaving the country intact and stable. As the new Ugandan government formed with Obote as its prime minister, Uganda appeared poised to avoid the bloody disruption that marked so many other African countries' transition from colonial rule to democracy.

Uganda's independence brought a sense of optimism to Ugandans. Black Ugandans who would be more sensitive to the customs and needs of their people now filled the highest governmental ranks, with the exception of a few British political and military advisers. The Ugandan people also looked forward to the KAR being administered by Ugandan officers rather than the British and to economic improvements for those working at menial jobs on plantations and in factories.

Ugandans celebrate independence from Britain in 1962.

The peace and stability, however, was short lived. Obote acquired a lust for power and used corruption to maintain that power. For Uganda, the road to decline began early at the hands of Obote. But Obote was not working alone. To shore up support from the new Ugandan army, he turned to Amin.

Obote saw in Amin potential for both good and evil. Because Amin had developed a reputation for brutal behavior, Obote decided to send him to Egypt to attend a training program for officers that emphasized tough yet compassionate treatment of soldiers. It was Obote's hope to moderate some of Amin's thirst for blood.

Quelling a Mutiny

There were some serious problems with the army following the changeover from British administration to self-rule. The British had promoted only a small handful of Ugandans, Amin being one of them, into the otherwise all-British officer ranks. The few British officers who remained behind as advisers worked in concert with Obote to bring more trained Ugandan soldiers into the officer ranks. In addition there was also a concern to improve the miserable pay and living conditions of the rank-and-file soldiers.

In 1963, one year after independence, Ugandan troops in one of the battalions demanded more pay than what they had received under the British.

Now that Uganda was under the control of a black Ugandan, these troops believed that they would receive better pay and have more opportunities for advancement. The new minister of defense, Felix Onoma, agreed to raise the pay of officers but not of the lower ranks. As the word spread, a fury raced through the army barracks in several

Amin as Sports Promoter

Sports in Uganda were well promoted during Amin's regime. Not only was Amin an avid athlete as a young man, but he was also a promoter and sponsor of Uganda's sports teams and individual athletes who performed well at international competitions. Amin took pride in Uganda's reputation as one of the best sporting countries in Africa during his rule.

Uganda's image as a sporting nation emerged in September 1972, in Munich, West Germany, when one Ugandan, John Akii-Bua, won the country's first-ever Olympic gold medal in the 400-meter hurdles. Knowing how significant the gold medal was to all Ugandans, Amin astutely honored the winner by naming one of Kampala's major streets after him. Amin went on to honor this hero as well as many others by throwing victory parties and handing out financial rewards.

When it came to rugby, Amin was especially popular with the Ugandan fans. During his dictatorship, he provided substantial material support for the national team, the Uganda Cranes. The Cranes played in three straight Africa Cup of Nations finals: 1974 in Egypt, 1976 in Ethiopia, and 1978 in Ghana, where they lost the final to the hosts. In 1976, after the team had qualified for the Africa Cup of Nations, Amin offered the Cranes the presidential jet to take them to Libya to go shopping.

In 1974 in Mexico, Ugandan boxer Ayub Kalule beat a West German boxer in the semifinals during the world's first Amateur Boxing Championship. He then beat a Bulgarian in the final to lift Uganda to fourth place among the world's best boxing teams. This achievement was enthusiastically received at home by Amin, who arranged a ticker-tape parade in Kampala followed by significant financial gifts to each team member.

cities. At the battalion location where the mutiny began, Onoma was chased by a band of soldiers, dragged from his car, beaten, and thrown into a stockade.

Terrified of being killed on the spot, Onoma personally promised to raise their pay. He then called the prime minister to report the mutiny and the deal that he had struck. Obote, sensing the volatile nature of this dilemma, sent for Amin, knowing he was one of the few Ugandan officers who commanded the respect of the troops. Amin, who was in Egypt, caught the next plane back to Kampala and reported to Obote.

From Obote's residence, Amin drove to the battalion where the mutiny had begun. Entering the barracks, he ordered all soldiers to line up at attention and then commanded them to cease their revolt. Walking up and down the line of men, he towered over each one intimidatingly while insisting that he would have no reservations about executing the entire unit if any one of them should dare to carry their mutiny any further. He also told them that there would be no raises. Knowing his reputation for fearsome treatment of anyone who defied his orders, the soldiers acquiesced and promised to return to their duties.

This incident convinced Obote that Amin was in fact capable of controlling his temper and that he wielded more authority over the army than any other man in Uganda. Obote, who continued to gain an unpopular reputation, real-

ized that without Amin to quell the disturbance, he might have been overthrown or killed. After dismissing several hundred of the mutineers, Obote expressed his appreciation to Amin by promoting him to the rank of colonel. According to former minister of health Henry Kyemba, "Obote had saved the man who was to eventually overthrow him. He did so because, at the time, Amin seemed indispensable."[15]

Moving Closer to Obote's Inner Circle

Obote had a tough decision to make. He feared Amin's violent tendencies yet appreciated his help in peacefully quelling the rebellious troops. Obote depended on the backing of the military to remain in power and saw Amin as the man who might be able to ensure troop loyalty. Caught in an ethical bind, Obote was forced to assess Amin's value either as his protégé, who would secure him the support of the army, or as an adversary, if he were to punish Amin for his savage behavior. At a critical juncture in 1964, according to Kenneth Ingram, "Obote recalled the warning of Sir Walter Coutts but opted to make Amin his protégé and rewarded him with yet another promotion to the rank of captain."[16]

For two years Obote experienced a cordial relationship with Amin, but in 1966 Amin's conduct again angered him. Amin caused a commotion one day when he walked into a Kampala bank with a solid gold ingot weighing

Lieutenant Colonel Amin (left) meets with African and British officers. Amin rose quickly through the military ranks.

166 pounds and bearing the stamp of the government of the Belgian Congo, which is modern-day Democratic Republic of Congo, and asked the bank manager to exchange it for $85,000 in cash. Word that Amin was involved in questionable activities quickly spread throughout Kampala.

Obote's political rivals investigated the incident. It emerged that the prime minister and a handful of close associates had used Captain Amin and units of the Ugandan army to intervene in a crisis in neighboring Belgian Congo. The investigation showed that these Ugandan troops were trading arms sup-

plies secretly smuggled to them by Amin in exchange for looted ivory and gold. Demands for Obote's resignation echoed across Uganda.

Amin's brash behavior placed him once again on Obote's list of assistants to be dismissed—but not for long. Opponents of Obote, who hoped to expel him from office, thought that Obote might be interested in sharing some of his authority with them in exchange for dropping the arms smuggling charges against him. The opposition hoped to add some of their members to the ministry responsible for the nation's education, transportation, commerce, military, and finance. Instead, Obote sent Amin and loyal troops to surround a palace where the opposition was meeting.

Obote stressed the importance of arresting the opposition without using violence, but Amin disobeyed his orders. The palace was defended by a small group of bodyguards armed only with rifles and shotguns. Amin arrived with his troops and set up heavy artillery around the perimeter of the palace. Reportedly eschewing so much as a warning or offer to surrender, Amin ordered the shelling of the palace. Exploding artillery shells tore through the palace walls and within minutes most of Obote's political opponents were dead. Amin claimed that he had killed forty-seven people, but an independent assessment placed the num-

ber at four hundred. As a reward for his troops, Amin allowed them to loot the palace while bodies were still being removed from the rubble.

At this point, Obote once again had grave misgivings about Amin. Yet, as had been the case in the past, Amin had gotten the job done; he had dealt with Obote's opposition. Besides, as Henry Kyemba points out in his book *A State of Blood: The Inside Story of Idi Amin*, "It seemed safe to trust Amin. He was, after all, nearly illiterate and showed no signs of political ambition."[17] Nineteen days later, Obote promoted Amin once again, this time to army chief of staff along with fellow Ugandan, Shabani Opolot. Amin was now coholder of the highest rank in the Ugandan army.

Chapter Three

BUILDING A BASE OF POLITICAL SUPPORT

By the late 1960s, Amin had more than one wife and at least fifteen children at home. He had met his first wife, Malyamu Kibedi, while serving as a sergeant in the KAR. The two had several children before being married in 1966. Another of Amin's wives, Kay Adroa, had comforted him during the gold ingot scandal. Amin also took on three other wives, which was permitted by Islamic law, as well as many mistresses. His family lived in high style, supported by his good pay as army chief of staff.

Still, Amin was not satisfied with his position. Obote, thinking that promoting Amin to army chief of staff would satisfy him, had underestimated Amin's appetite for power. This was a clear indication that Obote did not understand Amin, who had gained a remarkable sense of self-confidence first working under Obote and then alongside him. Rather than commit himself to his new position in the military, Amin gradually began to trade his soldier's uniform and rough language for the coat and tie and civil speech of a politician.

A Delicate Situation

Amin and Obote understood that each could be useful to the other as long as they could maintain a civil relationship. There was no friendship between the two, yet from Obote's point of view, he would continue in his role as prime minister while Amin commanded the army. But over the next five years, Amin was never willing to acknowledge Obote's supremacy. Beginning in late 1966, Amin started to build a base of support that would aid him when he finally snatched control of Uganda from Obote.

It was during this period that Amin revealed the cunning side of his personality. Now that he was close to Obote, Amin feigned support for the prime minister while plotting against him in the shadows. This remarkable cunning was identified by Denis Hills, a Uganda-based British subject who knew Amin well at this time. Hills astutely wrote of him as having "a successful tribal chief's qualities compensating for his lack of formal education: cunning, a talent for survival, personal strength and courage, and an ability to measure his opponents' weaknesses and his subjects' wishes."[18]

Both Obote and Amin understood that Obote's authority had been badly undermined first by the smuggling

As army chief of staff Amin built himself a loyal military following.

fiasco and then by the murder of his opposition at the palace. The key to holding power in Uganda, still shaky after the handover of authority from the British, was the army. Obote believed that he controlled the army because he had appointed Amin to command it. If Amin continued to disobey his orders or cause further scandal, Obote reasoned, he could remove Amin without jeopardizing his own political future.

Amin was equally aware of the connection between the prime minister's office and the army. To undermine Obote, Amin had only to turn the army's allegiance away from Obote and toward himself. Such a switch might occur if Amin could alter the tribal composition of the army to support him. He might, in effect, be able to construct his own personal army.

Building a Personal Army

During the mid-1960s, the Ugandan army consisted of a conglomeration of tribal warriors drawn from all regions of Uganda, some conscripted by the British and others by Obote's officers. Due to deep-seated intertribal rivalries, some warriors remained suspicious of members of their own units, weakening the army's effectiveness.

As army chief of staff, Amin began recruiting members of his own tribe, whose loyalties he could count on. The first unit he established was handpicked from members of his Kakwa tribe, who acted as his own personal bodyguards. Amin may have lacked formal education, but he was not a fool. He had observed other ambitious men cut down on the streets of Kampala since the departure of the British. His bodyguards always traveled with him, and they enjoyed a status above that of the soldiers of the Ugandan army.

To ensure that the rank-and-file soldiers were loyal to him and not to Obote, Amin awarded them better pay and provided improved equipment. To

Amin (far right) plotted a coup against President Obote (standing).

Amin paid his troops for loyalty with money earned from smuggling arms to rebel groups.

keep these bonuses from coming to the attention of Obote, Amin paid for them with money acquired from smuggling arms to rebels in Sudan and the Belgian Congo. To his soldiers, however, it appeared that Amin was paying for them out of his own pocket.

In addition to gaining the support of Ugandan troops, Amin purchased a small cadre of professional mercenaries loyal to him and no one else. This act, more than any other, suggested that he was thinking about a military takeover long before it would actually occur. Ac-

cording to historian George Ivan Smith, in his book *Ghosts of Kampala: The Rise and Fall of Idi Amin*, "Amin used troop barracks as a place for recruiting Nubian and Anyanya mercenaries who helped him to stage his coup."[19]

As 1969 drew to a close, Amin was a powerful man. He had assembled a significant army of bodyguards, mercenaries, and a growing number of Ugandan units whose allegiances now tipped more to him than to Obote. Partly funded by his own money acquired through smuggling and partly funded by the Ugandan treasury, Amin's military base was capable of rivaling that of Obote's.

Amin was keenly aware, however, that without international support his rule of Uganda would be short. He also knew that Obote was not endearing himself to British and Israeli interests because of his strong sense of Ugandan nationalism. Obote had promised when he became prime minister that he would eliminate as much foreign influence as possible to promote the political, social, and economic interests of Ugandans. To achieve that objective, Obote ceased complying with foreign business requests. For example, he denied British requests for Ugandan textiles and rubber. Such an attitude may have been a popular boost to Ugandan nationalism and the economy, but it alienated foreign businessmen and their governments, who had hoped to conduct business with Uganda. Also in keeping with Ugandan nationalism, Obote supported the replacement of Christianity, which had been introduced by the British, with Islam.

Seeking Foreign Support

By the end of the 1960s, Amin had established a secretive working relationship with the Israeli and British governments. Each wanted something different from Uganda, and each was willing to work through Amin while keeping Obote in the dark.

Some British were interested in running the plantations that they had established in the southern part of the country, where Obote had most of his supporters. Amin, whose support came from the north, was happy to open preliminary negotiations with British entrepreneurs and government officials. In exchange, the British agreed to make clandestine deposits into Amin's personal bank account, and this time, Amin threatened the bank president if news of his account activity were leaked to Obote. The British were pleased to find an ally and made their displeasure with Obote clear to Amin.

The interests of the Israelis were more complex. Amin had established friendships with the Israeli government when Israelis were training the new Ugandan army following the withdrawal of the British in 1962. Israel had a specific military interest in Uganda because of its immediate proximity to Sudan. The Israelis were interested in supplying southern Sudanese rebels with arms to fight a growing Muslim influence in the capital city of Khartoum. The Israeli objective was to encourage fighting between the rebels and Muslims, which would occupy Sudanese Muslim soldiers, at a time when Israel was under siege by other Muslim nations in the Middle East. A German arms smuggler named Rolf Steiner involved in this operation said in his autobiography, *The Last Adventurer*, "The Israeli interest in south Sudan was anything but humanitarian. By stirring up trouble in the area, they wanted to pin down a fraction of the Arab [military] potential. It meant that many less Muslim soldiers would bother them in Israel."[20]

The Israelis were aware of Amin's history of smuggling arms for gold and offered him a similar deal smuggling arms across the border to Sudanese Christians. The lure of gold was only one of Amin's motives for lending his support to the operation. Another was to involve his loyal followers living along the border in the smuggling operation so they too could profit. Amin knew that in appreciation, they would continue to support him against Obote. By promoting arms smuggling, yet never reporting the illegal activity to Obote, Amin was assuming responsibilities far beyond the scope of the army's chief of staff.

Because of Amin's operations, the Israelis were able to continue to supply the southern Sudanese liberation movement. Regarding Amin's role, Steiner notes that "although not all-powerful, he was strong enough to order his army to turn a blind eye to my smuggling service."[21]

Amin also needed to shore up support among his fellow Ugandans. His exposure to the public had been limited, and he now felt confident about meeting influential civic and religious groups without being accompanied by Obote. Such forays into the public infuriated Obote because they were inappropriate for a military commander and because Amin went without him. Obote sensed Amin's insolence but was helpless to stop him.

Internal Support

Amin sought to curry favor with Ugandans whenever possible. In 1969 a public

Amin meets with Israeli prime minister Golda Meir in 1971.

The Israeli-Amin Connection

When Radio Uganda announced at dawn on January 25, 1971, that Idi Amin was Uganda's new ruler, many people mistakenly suspected that Britain had a hand in the coup. However, telegrams exchanged between the British foreign offices in London and Kampala point to a more likely conspirator: Israel.

According to British sources, British high commissioner in Kampala, Richard Slater, bewildered by the coup, sought out Colonel Bar-Lev, the Israeli defense attaché, for more information. Slater found him with Amin; they had spent the morning of the coup together. Slater's next telegram to London discussed Bar-Lev's detailed understanding of several events that could only have been known to someone involved in the coup. Bar-Lev revealed that he had also spent the previous night with Amin, during which time Amin ordered the arrests of many officers in the armed forces who were sympathetic to Obote. He also detailed how all potential resistance had been eliminated throughout Uganda and, more importantly, in Kampala.

Equally noteworthy was Amin's first foreign trip as leader of Uganda: a state visit to Israel, not London. Amin arrived with what Israel's prime minister Golda Meir described as a shocking shopping list for arms that included small arms, tanks, helicopters, and even jet fighters.

According to political analyst Linda de Hoyos in her article "Idi Amin: London Stooge Against Sudan," Israel played a role in his coup:

> It is doubtful that Amin, without the urging of the Israelis, would have staged a successful coup in 1971. . . . Israel wanted a client regime in Uganda which they could manipulate in order to prevent Sudan from sending her troops to Egypt. . . . The coup succeeded beyond their wildest expectations. . . . The Israelis set up in Uganda a regime which pivoted in every respect to Amin, who in turn was under the strictest control of the Israelis in Kampala.

consecration of an Anglican bishop was held in northern Uganda. Obote intentionally did not accept his invitation to the high-profile ceremony because the Anglican Church was a British Christian institution and he feared his presence might suggest that he was pro-British rather than supportive of Ugandan nationalism. Amin, however, saw this as an opportunity to gather local support from those Ugandans who continued to support the church. Journalist

Judith Listowel attended the event and reported the awkwardness of a military leader attending a religious observance more appropriate for a prime minister: "There was General Amin drinking and making merry with his soldiers, right in the midst of the Prime Minister's camp."[22]

Amin attended Muslim ceremonies as well, publicly touting his Islamic faith. Shortly after the consecration of the new bishop, Amin attended a service at a mosque in the city of Kibuli, followed by many other services. One of his motives in attending daily prayers with his fellow Muslims was to impress upon them his commitment to keep Uganda free of British influence, even though he continued to work with the British clandestinely.

Amin attended other events to ingratiate himself to a variety of constituents. He was aware that his lack of formal education alienated him from Uganda's intelligentsia and that if he wanted to replace Obote and rule Uganda, he ought to court the university community. In 1970, with the awareness that Obote had chosen not to attend the graduation ceremony at Makerere University, Amin showed up wearing his military uniform.

Makerere was an academic showpiece for all of Africa. Established in 1922, it boasted the largest enrollment of any university in Africa and the most departments. Makerere was one of a small number of African universities popular with visiting faculty from Europe and America. Although Amin had not been invited to the graduation, he became the center of attention, and he took the opportunity to visit with students and faculty. He was even allowed to address the gathering, at which time, according to Henry Kyemba, "in a deliberate challenge to Obote, Amin made the comment, 'I fear no one but God.'"[23]

Secret Intelligence

By the late 1960s, Obote was intensely suspicious of Amin and excluded him from most of his meetings. Such exclusions, however, encouraged Amin to concoct other ways to gather information from informers within Obote's inner circle. Kyemba attests to Amin's ability to learn things not intended for him when he notes, "Amin's information service was good. His secret service contacts sent word of what was in the wind."[24]

Even when he was absent from Uganda, Amin received a steady stream of information about political events in Kampala. Historian George Ivan Smith reports this fact in his book *Ghosts of Kampala: The Rise and Fall of Idi Amin*, noting, "Amin clearly had an effective personal intelligence service operating for him in Uganda when he was abroad."[25] On more than one occasion, Amin was able to outmaneuver Obote because of information he had secretly received. In 1969, when Amin was in Israel, Obote seized the opportunity to collect information on him. Obote

Uganda's President Obote was unable to stop Amin from taking control of the country.

telephoned him, asking him to remain in Israel a few extra days on official business. Obote had been warned that Amin might be plotting to kill him and Obote wanted to search his offices looking for evidence that he could use to arrest him. Amin's intelligence notified him of the true intent of Obote's request, and Amin's return to Kampala the very same day was a shock to Obote, who had to immediately desist from his snooping.

In addition to high-level informants such as those within Obote's cabinet, Amin also needed the help of low-level agents willing to trade information for money, cigarettes, or alcohol. One such source of information were gangs called *kondos*, which were composed of young thugs who trafficked in weapons and other forms of valuable contraband. These gangs were a rich source of information about police activities throughout the country and, more importantly, in Kampala. Because *kondos* were often the target of police raids, they knew how the police operated and which officers would take bribes in exchange for useful information.

By late 1969 a combination of circumstances apparently moved Amin to attempt to eliminate Obote. Animosity between the two had boiled over and each had tried to undermine the other. In December 1969 Amin got wind of a political rally that Obote would be attending, and he allegedly sent assassins to kill Obote as he departed. Wounded from a gunshot in his mouth, Obote ordered an investigation while recovering in the hospital. Amin could not be found but turned up later at a meeting where Brigadier Okoya, the deputy army commander, indicated that Obote had entrusted him, Okoya, with the investigation. Okoya went on to say that two of the captured would-be assassins were being interrogated and that the net was closing in on the one believed to have planned the assassination. A date was set for a second meeting on January 26, 1970, when the guilty parties would be named and final decisions would be made about how to punish them.

Amin contacted as many of his informants as possible to determine what Okoya and the police knew. Soon, on January 25, shots were heard in the Kampala suburb where Okoya lived. Friends called police and went to the house to find Brigadier Okoya and his wife both dead from multiple bullet wounds. Nothing had been stolen, which indicated to the police that the killers had not come to rob them. That same evening, the two conspirators jailed following the failed assassination attempt were mysteriously found dead in a car that had been turned over and set on fire. No one was ever arrested for the murders, but most historians agree that Amin had ordered the attempt on Obote's life as well as the four other murders. George Ivan Smith asserts, "Captain Buweddeko, later a Brigadier under Amin, said that it was Amin who wanted Obote and Brigadier Okoya killed."[26]

Tightening the Noose

Amin's ability to create his own political base of support made him as powerful as Obote and perhaps even more so. For most of 1970, Obote recognized that Amin was a threat to his authority. Obote now knew that Amin had firmed up his control of the army but did not know the extent of it. To find out, he asked his intelligence committee to investigate. He learned that Amin was planning a military coup. This frightened him and mobilized him to take action to remove Amin from the army once and for all.

What Obote did not know, however, was that Amin had been tipped-off by informants and was preparing to confront Obote head-on. Obote sent two of his men to remove Amin from the army as quietly as possible. When they met with Amin, however, he launched into an out-of-control tirade and, according to historian David Gwyn, "Amin came prepared with a hand grenade, pulled the pin, and threatened to blow them all up if he were not left alone."[27] Unwilling to call Amin's bluff, the two men departed.

Idi Amin's ruthless tactics led to his seizing power in 1971.

what appeared to be fraudulent use of money, Obote ordered Amin to explain the financial irregularities one day before his departure for Singapore. Amin, however, knowing that Obote was preparing to leave, dodged the meeting.

Obote made arrangements with General Ojok to place Amin under arrest while Obote was in Singapore. He instructed him to act as soon as he departed from Entebbe Airport because he sensed that Amin was plotting against him as well. As Obote viewed the tense situation, who ever acted first would prevail over the other.

When Obote flew out of Entebbe Airport on January 11, 1971, he had already given Amin ample warning that he was finished as commander of the army. Amin, on the other hand, realizing that Obote's departure left him in command of the entire country, prepared to execute his own plans to eliminate Obote. In that sense, Obote had sealed his own fate by admonishing Amin yet failing to carry through with his threat to arrest him. As historian David Martin makes the case in his book *General Amin*, "When Obote flew out to Singapore, he had loaded the gun and pointed it directly at his own head. To survive, Amin had no other choice than to pull the trigger."[28]

Toward the end of 1970, Obote prepared to travel to Singapore for a few days. Unsettled about leaving the country and Amin behind, he tried once more to remove Amin from power. Obote had been advised that numerous military expenditures had exceeded reasonable amounts and that many had not been properly authorized. The amount in question, roughly $12 million, was a considerable sum, especially for a relatively impoverished nation. Hoping to seize on

Chapter Four

EMERGENCE OF THE TYRANT

As the wheels of Obote's plane lifted off the tarmac, both Obote and Amin set in motion plans to topple the other. When Obote arrived in Singapore, he telephoned his cabinet in Kampala asking General Ojok, "Has Amin yet been arrested?"[29] But when Ojok responded that the plan to arrest him was in progress and that Amin would likely be arrested by the next morning, Obote understood that the struggle was over; he had lost his bid to hold power. In a tense voice he then said to Ojok, "You're too late. Get out of the Parliament building. If you don't move now you will find it too late."[30]

Obote's dire warning was prophetic; with Obote stranded in Singapore, Amin had already seized his opportunity. Amin's private army swarmed through the streets of Kampala and down the roads and rivers of Uganda quickly suppressing all opposition while welcoming troops once loyal to Obote into Amin's camp. His loyal forces captured the heavy artillery and tanks controlled by Obote's forces and seized control of Uganda's few television and radio stations and the airport.

At this point, all of Uganda was under Amin's control, and the government was suspended. Amin's work over the previous few years—creating his own army, forming relationships with foreign governments, and attending many public functions—made him a popular alternative to Obote.

But Amin still had to contend with Obote, whose plane would soon be returning from Singapore. With the support of the army, Amin moved directly to assassinate him. Amin ordered a

Amin waves to cheering crowds after his successful coup.

model of Uganda's Entebbe Airport to be hastily built to determine where to position snipers so more than one would have a clean shot at Obote when he descended the steps of the plane's gangway. Fortunately for Obote, he had gotten wind of the coup over the radio and was able to depart the plane at a refueling stopover in Nairobi, Kenya, where he went into exile.

The Wolf in Sheep's Clothing

Immediately following the overthrow, much of the nation greeted Amin as a hero who had toppled an unpopular figure. Hoping for change and a better economy, crowds flooded the streets of Kampala and danced as soon as Amin's troops secured the capital city.

Although Amin had enemies, he had ingratiated himself to the public as a simple man, much like themselves, and promised to bring calm, stability, and prosperity back to Uganda. During Amin's first radio address to the nation, he sought to impress his simplicity upon Uganda's working class by emphasizing to them, "I am not a politician or an educated man but a professional soldier. I am, therefore, a simple man of few words."[31]

At this time, another of Amin's many personality characteristics emerged. Amin worked to calm public apprehension by clowning around, telling jokes, and laughing at problems to lessen their importance. By some people's standards, he sometimes behaved in a childlike manner. For example, he wore dozens of British war medals, which he had not earned, on his chest, causing his jacket to sag, and he declared himself King of Scotland. Amin had learned as a young boy in the British barracks that behaving like a buffoon was one way to disarm those who threatened him or those who felt threatened by him. Indeed, the international community laughed at his buffoonery.

Frivolities, however, would not calm the fears of educated professional politicians, who feared a massive bloodletting following the coup. To appeal to those who had not yet fled Kampala, Amin employed another ruse to reduce tensions. He claimed that he was willing to forgive his enemies and forge new friendships with those who had been

Amin's Inappropriate Behavior

Amin was legendary for his displays of inappropriate public behavior that, coming from a head of state, caused his nation embarrassment. Amin had a special knack for publicly humiliating others and himself at the same time. In July 1975 he had himself photographed sitting in a sedan chair borne on the shoulders of four skinny English businessmen wearing suits who had hoped to negotiate some business deals with Amin. Amin took the opportunity to create this bizarre parody of colonial images, only reversing the racial insult.

He loved, for example, to mock the foreign press and foreign heads of state. Amin once commented to Tanzanian president Nyerere that he would marry him if he were a woman. Amin was known to compose letters to Queen Elizabeth. In one letter he offered her a loan of 600 pounds, roughly $3,000, to help the ailing British economy that had a deficit of $3 billion, and in another he suggested to her that if she wanted to enjoy a wild time on the town some evening that she should visit him in Kampala. Amin also invited President Richard Nixon—during his political downfall at the height of his Watergate scandal that later led to his resignation—to come to Uganda by sending him a get-well card suggesting that he might enjoy a visit to Uganda for a much-needed rest.

Amin is carried by four Britons in a bizarre show of reverse racism.

loyal to Obote. Amin released many of Obote's civil administrators who had been jailed immediately following the coup. He even demonstrated his largess and equanimity by paying a few political and military leaders their back wages while they had been incarcerated.

Some Ugandans who had studied Amin's rise to power saw great contradiction in his sudden magnanimity. His kindness to remaining Obote loyalists and to the general population was out of character with the brutality that had made his rise to power possible. Historian David Gwyn, who had been living in Uganda prior to Ugandan independence and knew both Amin and Obote well, commented on Amin's benevolence following his coup: "This was Amin in the depths of deception. Far from being kind and considerate to a frightened population, he was acting as a wolf in sheep's clothing before moving in for the slaughter."[32]

Following a week of relative calm, Amin decided to eliminate potential threats still in Kampala. Brigadier Hussein and Lieutenant Colonel Ojok, both of whom had failed to arrest Amin when Obote departed for Singapore, and a few men of lower rank were dragged to a maximum security prison where they were clubbed to death with rifle butts, mutilated beyond recognition, and dumped in a ravine. So hideous were the beatings that historian David Martin commented, "They could only be identified by their tribal markings [tattoos]."[33] Amin, not wishing to provoke the population, publicly announced on the radio that the men were healthy when arrested and would soon be going home to their families.

The First Bloodletting

The dancing in the streets, spurred on by Amin's apparent willingness to forgive his enemies, did not last long. Although Amin's coup had cost the lives of relatively few opponents, it signaled the beginning of a wave of bloodletting throughout the nation. Over the next six months, the rate of murder by Amin's army and local police rose dramatically. Some of the killings were spurred by individual vendettas by Amin and his soldiers; others were aimed at tribes hostile to Amin's tribal connections, and yet others purged remaining members of Obote's inner circle that still posed a threat to Amin.

Amin moved to round up all remaining leading army officers and politicians sympathetic to Obote. Initially a group of thirty-six high-ranking politicians were brought to Kampala's central Makindye Prison, where they were sequestered in a cell separated from other prisoners. This separate cell had been named "Singapore" as a reminder of Obote's trip to Singapore that had provided Amin with his opportunity to strike.

Prisoners in another holding cell were able to peek through small chinks in the walls to witness the beginning of Amin's reign of terror aimed at anyone suspected of plotting his overthrow. According to eyewitnesses, Amin's troops entered the cell with wooden clubs and began breaking arms and legs. As the victims dragged themselves around the floor trying to fend off the blows, the soldiers poked and jabbed their bodies with bayonets. As the thirty-six men lay bleeding and in excruciating pain, witnesses said guards ordered the men to crawl out of the Singapore cell to a large armored personnel carrier that had backed up to a prison side door. Certain that they would be trucked out of town and murdered, the men refused to leave. At that moment, according to David Martin, who interviewed eyewitnesses:

The prisoners started shouting and wailing and then the cell door was thrown open and we saw three or four soldiers move into it. They started shooting and when they stopped after a couple of minutes there was not a sound except for the groans and screams from the wounded. Those who were still alive were killed with *panjas* [machetes] and were loaded into the armored personnel carrier.[34]

These horrific murders were but the first of many. After the Singapore cell

One of Amin's alleged enemies is readied for execution. The brutal dictator killed hundreds of thousands of his people.

was emptied, it was filled with the next load of Obote supporters. Soldiers repeated this brutal activity for days until the coagulating blood was so thick on the floor that other inmates were ordered to scoop it out with their bare hands.

Adding to the brutality of these killings were bizarre claims that Amin had practiced cannibalism on a few of the victims. Although such allegations may be nothing more than rumors, several people claimed they saw Amin eat small pieces of flesh from dead men he had known. When asked about the incident, Amin made the disturbing comment that he found them tasty. Historians are split on the matter. Some say that his comment was yet another example of his infantile behavior used to defuse tension. A few believe that he did practice cannibalism and that its basis may be found in the witchcraft practiced by his mother when Amin was a young boy.

Amin's brutality spread beyond Kampala. He became suspicious of officers from tribes loyal to Obote's tribe, especially those from the Acholi, Langi, and Itesot, which were positioned along the tense borders of Kenya and Tanzania.

Ruthless Restructuring of the Army

Amin had successfully swung the army in his favor prior to the coup, and now that he was in power, he could not afford to allow its allegiance to swing away. As a dictator who had grabbed power without an election and was holding it without constitutional authority, Amin understood that some units in the army remained hostile to his tribal connections and supportive of a possible return by Obote.

Of the dozens of tribes that composed the army, three of them had been considered by the British to be the most trustworthy: the Acholi, Langi, and Itesot. But these three tribes were not aligned with Amin's tribe, the Kakwa, and therefore, he believed, were not loyal to him. To replace them, Amin launched a major recruitment drive. Within three months, an additional ten thousand soldiers—whose loyalty to Amin would be assured—joined the army.

Roughly one half came from tribes along the Sudan-Ugandan border, where the Kakwa lived, and the other half from the west Nile area where Amin once lived with his mother before he joined the KAR.

To attract the new soldiers, Amin sent recruiters in trucks to remote tribal territories promising young men money;

After seizing power, Amin recruited soldiers solely from friendly tribes to assure their loyalty.

luxury goods such as radios, watches, and sunglasses; travel; and the excitement of big-city living. Thousands saw advantages in joining the army rather than herding goats and cattle across the dry landscape. Besides selecting soldiers tied to him by tribal and regional loyalties, Amin also selected Muslims over Christians in an attempt to distance Uganda from British influence. Although the entire population of Uganda was only 5 percent Muslim, 45 percent of newly enlisted soldiers were Muslim.

To make room for the new recruits and to speed up the restructuring of his personal army, Amin ordered the execution of thousands of soldiers, mostly from the Acholi, Langi, and Itesot tribes. Purging the army was one of the most gruesome examples of genocide practiced by Amin. He ordered the coordinated roundup of truckloads of soldiers who were driven to a variety of dumping grounds where they were executed. Tony Avirgan and Martha Honey, in their book *War in Uganda: The Legacy of Idi Amin*, report that, according to published records, an estimated five to six thousand Ugandan soldiers were murdered between May and July, 1971. They included 250 killed in the Mbarara Barracks, 120 killed at Moroto Barracks, 800 killed at Jinja Barracks, and 50 killed at Magamaga Barracks, and [also] at Moroto Barracks, 800 new recruits were machine gunned to death.[35]

The most notorious of the executions was that of the 800 soldiers from the Jinja Barracks. The men were trucked

Body Finders

Within one year of Amin's rise to power and the brutal killings that followed, thousands of family members failed to arrive home safely. At first, rumors spread that missing Ugandans were being held in detention camps or had been expelled to Kenya and Tanzania. Distressed and desperate families, waiting at police stations or hospitals for news of loved ones, sought help from members of a new profession that had sprung up in Uganda called body finders.

As the name suggests, body finders were people who took the name of a missing family member, tracked down the person's body, and returned it to the loved ones. The people who provided this macabre service worked for Amin, often members of one of his dreaded military organizations. Body finders typically worked in pairs and negotiated fees for their services ranging from $600 to $4,000, depending upon the missing person's position.

Once the price was paid, the body finders contacted those who would be most likely to know the whereabouts of the missing person. In most cases, they simply spoke with the highest-ranking members of PSU or the SRB secret police units. In exchange for some of the body finder's fee, information about the person's body condition and location would be revealed, the body retrieved, and finally returned to the family. In some cases, the fee was paid but the missing person was never located.

Amin's heartless regime charged citizens a fee to find the bodies of their murdered relatives.

to Karuma Falls, a waterfall on the Nile River a short distance from the city of Jinja. Their hands were bound behind their backs and their eyes blindfolded with cloth bags. Each was then taken to the water's edge, bayoneted once or twice, and pushed over the 145-foot-tall falls. Eyewitnesses say that all were probably still alive as they were swept over the falls to the rocks below. Some even claim that a herd of Nile crocodiles, attracted by the blood and commotion, congregated at the bottom of the falls and gorged on the bodies. Eyewitnesses further reported

that at one point, so many bodies were thrown over the falls that the remains temporarily clogged intake ducts at a hydroelectric power station at Jinja.

Amin's Dreaded Secret Police

Within six months of Amin's coup, rumors of his killing of political enemies and military units gradually drifted across the nation and throughout Kampala's neighborhoods. Witnesses to the murders in the jails and at Karuma Falls described the gruesome acts to friends and families who in turn passed the stories along to other Ugandans. Uncertainties about how much longer the murders would continue and how many more people would die strained the population, particularly families that felt they might be targeted. Fear along with eco-

nomic uncertainties that accompanied the ousting of Obote contributed to a gradual breakdown of basic services such as schools, hospitals, transportation, and businesses. As this crumbling cascaded over the next year, more and more

Amin's Arrogance

Arrogance was one of the hallmarks of Amin's regime. One of the most reported examples was Amin's penchant for wearing a military uniform loaded with British military medals from World War II. Not only had he not served in World War II, but as a non-British citizen he was not eligible to wear British war medals even if he had fought with the British. His jacket had to be lengthened to accommodate row after row of medals, yet even so, the look was comical because he wore so many that his jacket drooped from their weight.

While president of Uganda, Amin awarded himself the most revered British service medals, the Victoria Cross and the medal of the Distinguished Service Order. He also declared himself King of Scotland, a declaration that had all world leaders laughing. In keeping with the Scottish theme, Amin appeared at a Saudi Arabian funeral in 1975 wearing a Scottish kilt.

Besides his laughable uniform bedecked with unearned medals and his Scottish kilt, Amin's arrogance was manifested in letters to the Queen of England. One letter announcing a fantasy trip to London, which never occurred, appears in "The Words of the Honorable Field Marshal General Idi Amin Dada," on the *Bob Congress* Web site, which reads:

I am sending this message clearly, so that you will have ample time to prepare for what is required for my comfortable stay in your country. For example, I hope that during my stay there will be a steady supply of essential commodities because I know that your economy is ailing in many fields. Yes, Mrs. Queen, you better believe it. I am coming to London and no one can stop me. Whether you like it or not, I am bringing two hundred and fifty Ugandan reserve forces as my bodyguards. I want to see how strong the British are and I want them to see the powerful man from Uganda.

An excess of unearned medals and signs of office reveal Amin's arrogance.

citizens found themselves jobless and aimlessly wandering the streets.

Reluctant to frighten the population by filling the streets with rifle-bearing soldiers, Amin instead created secret police and undercover intelligence units that reported directly to him. Most notorious for their sinister activities were the Public Safety Unit (PSU) and the State Research Bureau (SRB), both of which, despite their misleading names, were instruments for spying, repression, and murder.

Their jobs included gathering information about Amin's potential rivals, controlling propaganda transmitted over television and radio stations, functioning as Amin's bodyguards, and eliminating threats to Amin by whatever means might be required. Although PSU members wore distinctive military uniforms that identified them as belonging to the PSU, members of the SRB operated undercover and often wore flowery, casual shirts, fashionable bell-bottom trousers, and sunglasses.

These organizations of repression became greatly feared by Ugandans in part because Amin failed to exercise tight control over them. There were so many officers, by some accounts three thousand, that they tended to act independently, carrying out whatever they believed needed to be done. Lacking restraint, within one year they were arresting and killing as many as seven thousand people a week for a variety of reasons. Some arrests and killings were motivated by arguments over personal property and girlfriends, some by false and malicious accusations, and others by old personal vendettas and animosities.

By late 1972 fathers and husbands mysteriously failed to return home from

The State Research Bureau

One of the most feared experiences by enemies of Amin was arrest by the State Research Bureau (SRB), a euphemism for Amin's goon squad. The SRB was at the heart of Amin's terror state and was responsible for the brutal murders of tens of thousands of Ugandans.

The SRB had its headquarters in Kampala, where a renovated prison served as a detention center, torture chamber, and place of execution. Guards who worked there, as well as a handful of political prisoners who were the fortunate few to be released, confirmed grisly stories of detainees who were forced to sledgehammer other prisoners to death, mistakenly believing if they did so they would be mercifully executed by a single bullet in exchange.

Prominent and anonymous citizens alike died at the hands of the SRB. Reasons for execution could include a soldier's desire for a victim's money, house, or women. Anonymous victims were usually shot or, at times, beaten to death, placed in a car, and pushed into a ditch to create the false impression that the victim had died in a car accident. More prominent victims, such as Anglican and Catholic clergy, former cabinet ministers, businessmen, and students, were publicly beheaded.

The BBC's African correspondent at the time, Brian Barron, entered the SRB shortly after the collapse of Amin's regime. On the Web site Islamonline, Barron wrote the article "Death of a Despot," in which he described his experience: "We stumbled down the stairs of the empty building into a charnel house [repository for the bones or bodies of the dead]. The floor was awash with blood, the bodies of the SRB's last victims lying in the darkness in their concrete dungeons."

work, and mothers and wives were brutally raped and murdered by Amin's uncontrollable secret police squads. Because most of these victims were not part of the political elite and because Amin controlled all forms of the media, few at that time recognized the magnitude of the problem. According to Henry Kyemba: "Their [the PSU and the SRB's] activities . . . comprise a merciless machine of terror that reaches into every corner of Uganda and seizes victims from the highest level of Ugandan society down to the lowest, at will and with impunity."[36] By the end of 1972, thousands of missing person reports were filed with Ugandan authorities.

Amin's initial reign of terror that cost the lives of tens of thousands of Ugandans temporarily came to an end after eighteen months. By August 1972 Amin and his terror units either had eliminated threats to his tyranny or ran them across the Kenyan or Tanzanian borders. Tragically, many Ugandans, most of them uninvolved in the politics of their nation, died as a result of the chaos that swirled around Amin and his brutal regime.

For reasons unclear to historians as well as to advisers close to Amin, he began to focus his sights on eliminating the last remnants of British colonialism. All Ugandans had experienced a surge of national pride ten years earlier when the British handed over the reins of power to Obote and his government. Now, Amin chose to complete the handover by expelling all remaining foreigners.

Chapter Five

EXPULSION OF THE ASIANS

After eighteen months of increasingly repressive rule, Amin made good on what is considered his only economic policy statement as ruler of Uganda. Amin had earlier announced that he would boost Ugandan national pride by ridding the nation of all foreigners and, in so doing, would stimulate the Ugandan economy. He believed that Ugandans would be just as capable, if not more so, of running their own economy than had the British and Asians. Believing that he had already eliminated his most threatening opponents and that Obote lacked the support necessary to return, Amin now turned his gaze toward the seventy thousand or so Asians living in Uganda. Although they were collectively called "the Asians," all were from the Asian subcontinent of India. This ethnic group for the previous century had been controlling Uganda's economy under the British. In late 1972, in a move to purify Uganda's population and to elevate Uganda's image in Africa as a new and self-reliant emerging nation, Amin ordered the expulsion of the entire Asian population.

Many decades before Amin, during the height of British colonial ambitions in Africa, the British installed thousands of British subjects in prime economic positions to regulate most of the Ugandan economy. As the business class in Uganda, they occupied a social and economic niche below the British colonial authorities but above the Ugandans. Whether managing plantations, running small retail businesses, taking charge of Uganda's banking system, or controlling imports and exports, the Asian business class profited handsomely.

The presence of the Asians was a source of widespread animosity for Ugandans. The lifestyle of the Asians in Kampala who drove cars, educated their children in British schools, and enjoyed comfortable living in the finer houses was far better than that of most Ugandans.

Amin was keenly aware that Ugandans held a deep-seated resentment toward the Asians because of their financial success. As an example of the inequity between Ugandans and Asians, historian George Ivan Smith tells this revealing story about Sundays in Kampala:

Asians grasp for immigration forms after Amin expelled them in 1972.

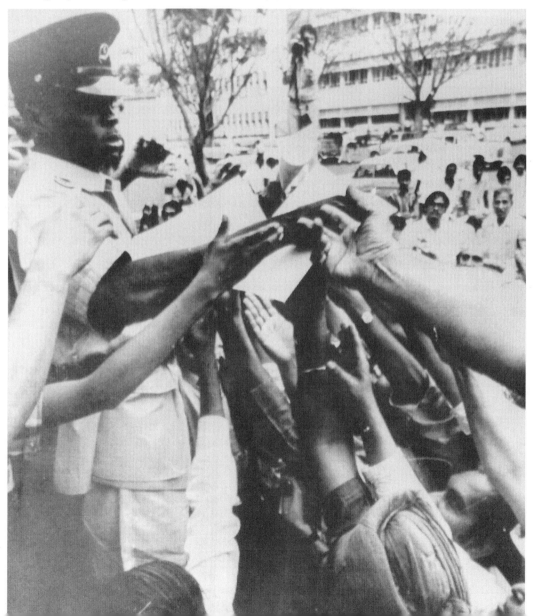

Exiled Asians

The tragedy of forced exile for Uganda's Asian population went beyond the loss of businesses and family bank accounts. The simple acts of booking passage out of Uganda, clearing Ugandan customs, and boarding planes to either Britain or India were filled with risks.

Interviews with departing Asians revealed horrors right up to the boarding of planes. In a few cases, departing women were separated from their families and raped in secluded rooms and men beaten before their families for no apparent reason. All were searched for money or other valuables. To avoid the seizure of family jewelry, necklaces and rings were worn by teenage girls and even younger ones who were less likely to be searched. In some cases, the gems were removed from settings and sewn into the hems of dresses. In all cases, the moment of passing through customs was quite tense since discovery would have been disastrous.

Once through customs, some families faced separation. It was not unusual for members of the same family to hold passports from different countries. Most Asians held either Indian or British passports, and parents with different passports were not allowed to depart on the same plane to the same country. Generally any children were allowed to depart with their mothers. In the story "1972: Life after Idi Amin," found on the BBC News Web site, Nemish Mehta was forced to flee to India on his mother's passport and to wait eighteen months to reunite with his father in Britain. He recalled many years later:

> I remember the overwhelming sense of momentous parting from each other. Too young to understand the danger, I and my brothers and sisters saw only the actions which our elders took to try and salvage whatever they could. It took 18 months of effort to be allowed into the UK [Britain]. My memory is of a not very friendly environment [in Uganda]. Of course, as a young child, we would not have experienced the worst of the racism and abuse.

On Sundays, every Asian would get into a motor-car—Africans did not have motor-cars then—and they would drive very slowly in a caravan of cars, three miles long, with as many as eight or nine people in each car, and they would get out and sit on the grass. The Africans would just stand and watch them.[37]

Amin knew that his expulsion order, which capitalized on economic and racial tensions resulting from the

Asians' higher standard of living, would be popular with his countrymen. Amin explained his decision before a gathering of black Ugandans, most of whom wore military uniforms, saying, "Asians have kept themselves to themselves and as a community have refused to integrate with Africans. Their main interest has been to exploit the economy. They have been milking our economy for years and now I say to them all—Go!"[38]

Claiming that God came to him in a dream and told him to make Uganda a black man's country, on August 7, 1972, Amin ordered Asians out of the country and ordered the seizure of their extensive property holdings. Confiscated property included 5,655 businesses, numerous factories and farms, and an additional $400 million in personal savings held in Ugandan banks. He then gave the Asians ninety

Asian exiles arrive in the United Kingdom from Uganda.

days to exit the country and made clear his resolve to oust them by commenting, "If you don't go by then, I will make you feel as if you are sitting on fire."[39] Amin insulted the British government by notifying Queen Elizabeth II, whom he addressed as "Mrs. Queen," that they would not be allowed back.

The ninety days that Amin allowed for the Asians' departure was hellish. Families asked for more time so they might sell their businesses, some of which had been in families for four generations, but few Ugandans offered to buy. Asian families were torn emotionally because many had lived their entire lives in Uganda although they held either British or Indian citizenship. Some families in which the parents held passports of different nations learned that they would be separated because they would depart on different planes to different countries. Even before the Asians departed, their shops were looted, their automobiles stolen, and some were ridiculed while walking the streets of Kampala. According to historian David Martin in his book *General Amin*, Amin's brutality followed them on their way out: "The Asians were treated brutally as they left Uganda. Some were killed by Amin's marauding troops. They were harassed, manhandled, robbed, and a few raped. They were forced to leave all their property behind with their businesses."[40]

When their ninety days had expired, all Asians departed with empty pockets for either India or England.

Abandoned were the well-regulated business and financial institutions that had contributed greatly to Uganda's reputation as the Pearl of Africa.

Paying Off the Military and Business Elite

Amin had a plan for the abandoned Asian businesses. As 1973 began, it was clear that his first two years of rule had produced no positive results. His administration had descended into a tyranny of spies and secret police, public services were collapsing, the streets were chaotic, and people were debilitated because of fear. To solidify his authority within the swirl of instability, Amin conceived the idea of distributing the businesses as incentives and rewards to key individuals loyal to him.

His most important supporters were the military and a handful of emerging Ugandan businessmen who had assisted the Asians and had at least a rudimentary understanding of business administration. Among these businessmen was a core in Kampala and another core of farmers who owned small plantation holdings throughout the country. Amin understood that his hold on power would be short unless he were able to appease these leaders.

The highest-ranking officers in the Ugandan army were awarded the homes and cars abandoned by the Asians in return for their loyalty. Amin selected men from several Nubian tribes from northern Uganda, such as his own Kakwa

Amin and Ugandan Nationalism

To many Ugandans, the expulsion of the Asians was a symbol of Uganda's nationalism. Amin stressed during his announcement of the expulsion that one of his principal motives was to rid Uganda of all nonblack people. His motive was to uplift the spirits of all Ugandans, and other black Africans as well, by proving that his nation could prosper without the assistance of Europeans and Asians.

Amin's rise to power partly symbolized the revival of black nationalism. Many historians point to it as one of the reasons he was able to maintain power within Uganda despite his reckless murdering and torturing of anyone who might oppose him. From the point of view of many Ugandans, no matter how misplaced Amin's priorities or vicious his misdeeds, he at least stood up to the whites and the Asians.

Amin enjoyed expressing his sense of superiority over the British when he publicly humiliated them. There were many photographs taken during such moments. One was a photograph of the president at a news conference pointing his finger menacingly at a group of British journalists while expelling them from Uganda for stories they had written critical of him and which challenged his knowledge of international diplomacy. On another occasion Amin staged a publicity stunt for the media, forcing British diplomats, still working in Kampala before their withdrawal, to kneel before him and recite an oath of loyalty.

What often appeared to the British to be Amin's ineptitude was a source of amusement and pride to fellow Ugandans. Writer Denis Hills understood that Ugandans took pride in seeing their president humiliate the British because of the racial and economic humiliation they had suffered under British colonial rule. In his article "Idi Amin Dada Oumee," on the Moreorless Web site, Hills captures Amin's dream shared by all Africans to be free of foreign dominance: "It is not enough to dismiss Amin as a buffoon or murderer.... He is an African reality. He has realized an African dream. The creation of a truly black state."

tribe, who could be trusted with greater certainty than could tribes from southern Uganda, where Amin was viewed with suspicion.

Initially the rewards worked as planned. The cars and homes commandeered from the Asians provided their new occupants a higher level of comfort and status than they had ever before experienced. Some of Amin's generals and cronies had indoor plumbing and electricity for the first time. Automobile caravans to Kampala's parks on Sundays became a major event, signifying the independence of Ugandans.

For those who now enjoyed a higher standard of living, Amin was a national hero. Their loyalty to him strengthened as did their obligations. They clearly understood that if they wished to continue enjoying their new trappings of luxury and success, they would need to repay Amin with their unflinching allegiance. The expulsion of the Asians also made Amin the champion of those who remained among the poorest of Ugandans. They now had, for the first time, hope for a better future in which they too might one day drive a car or enjoy a home.

A Bitter Reality

In a short time, however, what had been an enjoyable fantasy quickly became a bitter reality. Most of the cars fell into a state of disrepair because Asian-owned repair shops closed and auto parts ceased to flow into the country. By the end of 1973, most autos were abandoned or sold as scrap to junkyards. In some neighborhoods in Kampala, they were simply abandoned on the streets. Similar problems occurred with the homes, which also required maintenance unfamiliar to Ugandans. As water pipes broke, roofs leaked, or electrical fuses failed, the difficulties of modern living set in.

The high-ranking officers and favored Ugandan businessmen had no idea how to maintain their newly acquired houses. They had even less understanding about how to run their newly acquired businesses because under the Asians, the Ugandans had only acted as assistants and therefore had only elementary business skills. According to George Ivan Smith, the manner of redistribution of Asian-owned businesses was not based on a recipient's experience but was done recklessly without thoughtful consideration:

> Amin handed over the hotels and the shops to his own soldiers. There are photographs of him walking down the street with a bunch of his officers around him, plus a civil servant with a notebook. It was, "Right, give that one to Brigadier So-and-So, and give this to Brigadier somebody else."[41]

The shop owners honored the old respected tribal value of sharing by inviting their relatives to take whatever they wanted. Within weeks of the handover of shops and businesses, many new owners stood staring at empty shelves not understanding that such expressions of family and tribal loyalty were a costly mistake when running a business. Without rudimentary business understanding about the flow of goods, credit, inventories, international currency fluctuations, and price structures, shop owners saw their businesses quickly falter, just like the automobiles and homes.

Ugandans peer into closed shops formerly run by expelled Asians.

Economic Decline Under Amin

While the expulsion of the Asians was initially popular, many Ugandans had second thoughts as the country sank into a quagmire of economic chaos. With the departure of the Asians, utter economic failure followed close behind. In general, few Ugandans understood how to operate plantations, run and repair machinery, weave clothing, harvest and process sugarcane, or preserve fish for export. Equally hard hit were the retail businesses.

Lacking experience buying and selling retail goods that ranged from imported foods and clothing to electronics and furniture, prices fluctuated widely—shopkeepers did not know what to charge for items. In many cases, they had no choice other than to ask customers what they had paid in the past for their purchases and to accept whatever the customers told them. One of the more egregious examples of mismanagement and confusion was shop owners selling imported shirts mistakenly believing that the collar size sewn on the shirt labels was the price tag.

Following one economic debacle after another, shop owners either did not know how to order more stock or lacked the money to do so, and shortages of essential commodities plagued Kampala. As shops ran out of goods, the prices began to escalate as more and more people competed to purchase fewer and fewer supplies. As the spiral of escalating shortages and higher prices continued, fighting broke out among shoppers trying to purchase, and in some cases to steal, the last remaining goods on the shelves.

By the end of 1973 the entire supply system collapsed. This disaster fostered a black market that favored those with the most money, leaving very little for the vast majority of poor Ugandans. For the poor, the collapse translated into hunger and anger as mobs of Kampalans chanced being arrested by roaming the streets looting stores. Amin, whose understanding of the economy was as elementary as that of many of his advisers, moved to address the problem in Kampala at the expense of rural regions. Amin ordered goods slated for rural distribution rerouted to Kampala and other cities with large populations, such as Jinja, Entebbe, and Masaka. Scarcity was partially relieved in the major cities, but basic foods such as butter, milk, and bread remained in short supply, while construction materials; fuel for running buses, trains, and factories; and critical medicines became almost impossible to find.

Compounding these economic woes was Amin's continuing need to finance his military and secret police units. Amin spent heavily on rifles, artillery, tanks, and an assortment of military supplies to strengthen his personal army. Initially he paid cash for arms, but later, foreign governments such as Britain and Israel loaned him money. By the end of 1973 and the beginning of 1974, however, foreign governments recognized the extent of his economic fiasco and refused requests for more loans to pay for armaments. Israel at this time had already lost an estimated $30 million dollars in unrecoverable loans.

Many historians consider the expulsion of the Asians to have been the death knell of Amin's reign. Not as oppressively cruel as the execution of thousands of Ugandans, it was, however, the one decision that shattered the economic backbone of the nation, causing it to spiral into chaos from which it never recovered. The chaos and ensuing poverty only served to initiate another wave of repression by Amin's secret police frantically trying to regain some semblance of order. The one positive outcome of this series of tragic events was that it drew the attention of an international audience of leaders and newspapers, notifying the world that something was terribly wrong in Uganda.

Loss of International Support
Uganda's plunging economy combined with Amin's failure to provide any effective government policies eventually

The United States and Amin

During his reign, Amin never experienced a diplomatic relationship with any of the three American presidents—Richard Nixon, Gerald Ford, or Jimmy Carter—although he received American foreign aid. His coup occurred under the presidency of Richard Nixon in 1971, but the president took no action because Obote was known to be corrupt and Amin was still unknown, as were his possible policies. But when Amin expelled the Asians, the Nixon administration formally severed diplomatic relations between the United States and Uganda.

The Ford administration's anti-Amin stance took the form of pretending to assist him. In December 1986, the *New York Times* reported that agents of the Central Intelligence Agency had provided bombs,

Jimmy Carter was the first U.S. president to speak out against Amin's regime.

military equipment, and training to Amin in 1975. The United States also provided special police training to high-ranking officers in Amin's SRB and PSU secret police units.

A government official's explanation for assisting the secret police was that the United States believed that it could control and manipulate Amin by providing him with arms and establishing a false sense of friendship. Once the false friendship was established, the United States might then use the promise of future arms shipments in exchange for policies of value to the United States. Noted in Steven Niven's article "Idi Amin: Crazy Like a Fascist," on the Africana Web site, government officials said, "By training Amin's men, we were able to have some influence over Amin."

It was not until the Carter administration that any president publicly spoke out against Amin's brutality. Contained in "Dictator Idi Amin Dies," on the BBC News Web site, President Jimmy Carter said, in noting Amin's mounting toll of human rights abuses, that his policies "disgusted the entire civilized world."

attracted international attention. Even nations that had not loaned Uganda money, such as the United States and many European nations, were increasingly concerned with the country's growing economic collapse, poverty, and repression. Britain and Israel, at one time ardent supporters of Amin, now turned their backs on him. As Julius Nyerere, president of Tanzania, described the circumstances in 1974, "If the people of Uganda thought that they were in the frying pan during Obote's time, they knew they were in the fire during Amin's."[42]

To compensate for the loss of loans and imports from previously friendly countries, Amin began to build alliances with leaders of predominately Muslim nations who shared his support for the religion while opposing Christianity brought by the ousted European colonial powers. Many saw his alliances with Middle Eastern and North African nations as glaring contradictions of his pledge to Ugandan nationalism. Muslim nations, however, were willing to enter into business ventures with Amin but only on a small scale and quite reluctantly. And even then, only those Muslim nations with particularly strong anti-Israeli sentiment such as Libya, Iraq, Egypt, and Saudi Arabia were forthcoming. The leaders of these countries applauded the anti-Israeli stance Amin took after Israel severed support for him. According to Henry Kyemba, in his book *A State of Blood: The Inside Story of Idi Amin*, "After the [1972] Munich Olympics massacre of Israeli athletes, he declared his joy at the slayings, adding that he admired Hitler for 'burning the Israelis alive with gas in the soil of Germany.'"[43] Four years later, in a letter Amin sent to United Nations secretary-general Kurt Waldheim, Amin said, "Germany was the right place when Hitler was Prime Minister [chancellor] and supreme commander. He burnt over six million Jews."[44]

Libya and Egypt stepped forward to offer some token assistance to the beleaguered Ugandans. Both of these countries viewed loans as a waste of their money but felt a humanitarian obligation to lend some support for fellow Muslims. But what Amin and Uganda needed most were trained business leaders. They refused to go to Uganda, however, fearing they might be the next to be pushed over Karuma Falls or discovered dead in a crumpled automobile.

Lacking a healthy economy while continuing to be terrorized by Amin's secret police, the average Ugandan living in Kampala and other large cities was being squeezed out of existence. What little money Amin could find went to his henchmen to maintain order while the streets of Kampala and other cities were turned into a network of thievery.

Urban Chaos

In September 1974, police reported a rather odd theft. Weighing two hundred pounds each and having no value other than covering holes in the streets that give workmen access to sewer and water pipes, several solid iron manhole covers from Kampala streets were reported missing. The police were baffled. Vanishing too from the city's streets were public telephones; bus benches; light bulbs from street lights; iron handrails on staircases; sections of iron fences; a large number of cars; and soap, paper towels, and toilet paper from public restrooms.

The Kampala zoo reported the theft of exotic animals. Initially missing were monkeys and small mammals but later zebra, gazelle, and other animals followed. One by one, people reported finding charred animal skeletons scattered throughout Kampala's poorest neighborhoods. Eventually, the zoo closed and the remaining animals either starved to

Amin told UN Secretary General Waldheim (right) that he admired Hitler's murder of the Jews.

death or were killed in their cages, butchered, and the meat passed through the bars to starving family members.

At roughly the same time, microscopes began disappearing from Mulago Hospital's blood laboratory as did all of the hospital's ambulance tires. The main post office lost dozens of uniforms, while electrical pumps from gas stations disappeared along with the sheet metal roofing from train stations. Restaurants resorted to serving meals with plastic plates, cups, and utensils because all ceramic and metal tableware was stolen. As Henry Kyemba observed in his book *A State of Blood: The Inside*

A Psychological Profile

Amin's mental imbalance has been the subject of many articles by psychologists, historians, writers, and acquaintances. One writer, E.B. Idowu, provides this psychological profile in his article "Idi Amin, the Little-Big Man: Thoughts on His Life and Death," on the Out of Africa Web site:

Idi Amin was a big man, size wise, but in reality a small man of heart. He pursued power, women, fame, he desired to be loved by the people of Uganda, only to be despised and rejected. A man deeply insecure that wanted to be taken seriously but often was seen as a bumbling buffoon who never saw that with the titles he gave himself came responsibilities. He wanted to be served, but in turn never learned to serve those whom he presided over. He became a laughing stock even in his own country, so he resorted to naked, abusive power, terror and fear to subjugate a country. He went through life as an intimidator, even British citizens had to bow to him and pledge allegiance. He wanted to be seen as a great statesman and wrote letters of advice to President Nixon at the time of Watergate, asked Queen Elizabeth to come to Kampala and find a real man, him. He offered himself to be King of Scotland, thank God, that was turned down.

When you study the life of Idi Amin, you see a life that was corrupted by power. Power that ran amok, power that was not harnessed, but allowed to reign freely subjugating a people who wanted a servant leader, but got a tyrant, twice the son of hell that Milton Apollo Obote had been, the President of Uganda that Idi Amin overthrew. He called himself big Daddy, the one who never had a father around him. His father abandoned the family soon after Amin was born near the Sudanese and the Democratic Republic of Congo somewhere around 1925.

Amin enjoys roast chicken at a parade commemorating his military coup. Meanwhile, many of his people starve to death.

Story of Idi Amin, "In addition to terrible shortages, everything that can be stolen is stolen."[45]

Urban chaos had descended on Kampala. Historian David Martin writes, "[Amin] passed a decree empowering his guards to shoot on sight anyone suspected of having or being about to commit a theft."[46] As a reward, they were allowed to keep all stolen goods confiscated from the dead thieves, or those about to become thieves. The result of this reckless policy resulted in the deaths of thousands more innocent people. Yet, at the same time, stolen goods were never returned to the legal owners. The culprits turned out to be the poorest people, who could neither count on receiving favors or gifts from Amin nor could they find employment in a collapsing economy in which unemployment was rampant.

After four tragic years, Amin's reckless rule was no longer passively accepted by many Ugandans. Because of the growing suffering experienced by most segments of the population, pockets of resistance to Amin's rule gradually surfaced. Some people began to talk openly about killing their leader.

Chapter Six

Rooting Out Internal Opposition

By 1975 Amin's rule had spiraled downward, causing widespread internal opposition to surface. After several years as the head of state, Amin had provided no foreign policies, economic solutions, or social programs for the betterment of Ugandans. Although Obote had been widely disliked, Amin was now widely hated. In a very short time, Uganda's international reputation as the Pearl of Africa had been eroded by widespread economic and social decline, human rights violations, and a growing debilitating climate of fear.

Amin had a predilection for blaming all of his country's problems on outsiders, especially Obote, who had been living in Kenya and Tanzania since the 1971 coup. In truth, however, most of the opposition to his tyrannical rule came from within Uganda. Those willing to risk their lives by speaking and acting out against him included women's groups, plantation workers, students and faculty at Makerere University, respected religious leaders, and even the military.

As had been the case in the past, rather than resolve the genuine concerns and complaints of his people, Amin viewed them as threats. Acting to shore up a crumbling regime, Amin lashed out against the complaints of his people until they were either subdued or eliminated. For the next two years, Amin launched his second wave of brutality as horrific as the one that immediately followed his coup.

Punishing Complaining Farmers

The instability caused by Amin's rule was most noticeable in Kampala but

Accusations of Cannibalism

Of the many disparaging charges that Amin faced, that of cannibalism was always the most bizarre, disgusting, and disputed. Other dictators might describe their enemies to be insurgents, threats, or terrorists, but only Amin is reputed to have once described a person as being "tasty."

Charges of cannibalism surfaced several times during Amin's tyranny. After his coup over Obote, Amin rounded up the military leaders that did not support the coup, murdered them, decapitated some, and allegedly sat their disembodied heads around the presidential dining table. He then scolded them for not supporting him, while allegedly taking bites out of them.

Some who knew Amin, along with some historians, find the accusations questionable. According to Steven Niven, author of the story "Idi Amin: Crazy Like a Fascist," on the Africana Web site: "There is no concrete evidence that Amin was a cannibal. He did once tell reporters who asked him about the rumors of cannibalism that he had tried human flesh and it was too salty. That statement may have been true. It may also have been one of Amin's many weapons of mass distraction—the only weapons he had when it came to dealing with the world's major powers."

Not everyone, however, is quick to dismiss the charges. Some Ugandans familiar with various forms of witchcraft point to Amin's exposure to animal mutilations, bloodlettings, and blood tasting used by his mother, Assa. After Amin's exile to Saudi Arabia, one of Amin's guards, Abraham Sule, told a disturbing anecdote suggesting a witchcraft connection. He reported in the story "A Clown Drenched in Brutality," that "[Amin] put his bayonet in the pot containing human blood and licked the stuff as it ran down the bayonet.... Amin told us: 'When you lick the blood of your victim, you will not see nightmares.' He then did it."

eventually it extended into rural agricultural areas. One example was the increasing tendency for farmers, who accounted for 85 percent of the population, to switch from growing cash crops, such as cotton, sugarcane, coffee, and tea, to subsistence crops such as beans, grains, and vegetables. Trading partners that historically had purchased these crops—Western European nations, Israel, and the United States—refused to trade with Uganda for reasons of unpaid outstanding loans and to protest Amin's brutality toward his own people. Farmers who could no longer get a fair price for lucrative cash crops uprooted them because they could no longer feed their families. By planting subsistence crops, they ensured that their families would be able to eat in the faltering economy. As one Ugandan economist explained the situation, "Subsistence production was the peasant's response to Amin's urban tyranny."[47]

Cash crops, which were used as exports for trade, were the few exports that Amin was counting on to keep the stumbling economy from falling to its knees. According to comprehensive market reports, all of Uganda's agricultural and industrial production declined precipitously by 50 percent between 1971 and 1978.

Amin's response to this economic problem was to instill fear in the farm-ers. In 1976 he decreed that each farmer had to plant at least two acres of cotton. Soldiers were sent out to enforce the decree, and those failing to comply were shot. Most farmers obeyed, but their opposition surfaced as many refused to weed the cotton, which then shriveled and died. Not only did valued exports fall, but also the number of acres under productive cultivation declined.

When Amin learned how the farmers had fooled him, he exploded in a rage. Farmer opposition was strongest in a region called Buganda, in the southern part of the nation where tribes had always hated Amin. To deter any future disobedience, Amin sent his army through villages, indiscriminately killing farmers. Estimates of the

The cruel dictator was accused of many atrocities, including cannibalism.

number of dead range between four and eight thousand.

Anger over the killings spread to agricultural workers throughout the country. Workers at several processing plants went on strike to voice their opposition to Amin's brutal policies. For striking workers at the Lugazi Sugar Works, for example, punishment was light the first time; their biweekly allocation of ten pounds of sugar, part of their compensation, was terminated. But when that failed to send the workers back to work, soldiers entered the factory, broke up the union, and killed its leaders. In retaliation, sugarcane plantation workers set fire to thousands of acres of sugarcane, further reducing Uganda's cash crop exports and prompting another wave of killings by Amin's soldiers.

The farmers were not alone in their opposition to Amin. Much of the remaining opposition came from the university community in Kampala, where poverty was at its worst and crime was out of control.

Attacks on the University

Although Amin once tried to curry favor with Uganda's intelligentsia, most of whom were associated with the nation's largest and most prestigious university, Makerere University, he was never accepted by them. Largely uneducated and mistrustful of academics, Amin now made no attempt to mask his irritation and disdain for faculty members and students, most of whom

he viewed as having enjoyed greater privilege growing up than he had.

Amin pompously declared himself chancellor of the university, a title normally reserved for a revered faculty member, and a title Obote never assumed. Such arrogance angered both faculty and students, most of whom opposed what they perceived to be his irresponsible and repressive despotism. In addition, university personnel resented a national leader with, at best, a fifth-grade education and whose behavior was now frequently described as demented and embarrassing.

Amin then angered the university even more by charging his minister of defense with the job of determining who would be admitted to the university. According to historian David Gwyn, Amin made this unprecedented move because "merit comes well behind religion and tribe as a qualification. So the education of the future is pointed in whatever direction Amin wants and it's not in the direction of the majority of Ugandans."[48]

In 1976, in response to Amin's interference in university affairs and his reign of terror, students at Makerere University held rallies on campus demanding his resignation and a return to constitutional rule. Initially Amin merely refused to allocate any further funds to the university for maintenance, faculty salaries, or laboratory equipment and supplies. Later, however, anti-Amin demonstrations spilled over into the streets of Kampala. As a sea of students poured down the streets, residents joined the surge until an estimated ten thousand Ugandans vented their anger by tearing down Amin posters and chanting for his resignation.

Once demonstrators returned to campus, Amin set loose squads from the SRB. When the SRB arrived on cam-

pus, eyewitnesses reported that they surrounded the demonstrators. According to the eyewitnesses:

The students were tortured, arms and legs were broken, and the soldiers forced them to crawl on jagged concrete paths. The attacks went on into the night. The Dean confirmed

The Tragedy of Makerere University

The oppressive rule of Amin extended to Uganda's academic jewel, Makerere University. Amin's lack of education made him suspicious of anyone with a university degree and unwilling to support the university, which he perceived to be a subversive institution.

On a hill a local king called Makerere, meaning "cradle of the infant sun," the British built one of black Africa's most famous universities in 1921. The university was founded as a technical school with five instructors. In 1949 Makerere became a college associated with the University of London, and in 1963 the nucleus of the University of East Africa. For close to a half century, some of East and Central Africa's best minds were educated at Makerere University, which offered degrees in politics, business, science, the arts, and medicine.

Then came Amin's rule. Amin imposed his brutal dictatorship, and, like much of Uganda, Makerere withered. During the 1970s, hardly a building was constructed or repaired. Neglect was evident throughout the university as walls and floors of many buildings began to crack and paint was peeling off. Lecture hall benches, chairs, and desks were sold for firewood, aging laboratory equipment in need of replacement fell into disrepair, and the medical school lost crucial British accreditation.

Events at Makerere got even worse; faculty came under attack by Amin and his administrators. Several foreign professors and visiting professors were expelled from the country following allegations of inciting an uprising against Amin's regime. Following continuing contentious relations between the university and Amin, the president of the university was found murdered in his car. By the end of Amin's reign, the university had ceased functioning.

As self-appointed Makerere University chancellor, Amin wears the robes of office.

that women students were raped. . . . More than five hundred students were taken to various prisons. Many were beaten but most were returned. University records indicate that the number of dead reached one hundred but others [estimate] as low as two or three. [49]

Following the brutal beatings, and fearing for their lives, many fled while foreign students booked passage home. Not all abandoned the university, however. Some continued their studies even as funding ran out and tensions contin-

ued. Meanwhile, police brutality erupted sporadically.

Sympathetic faculty members were treated no better. Many foreign faculty members fled or were detained by police, forced onto planes, and deported. Ugandan instructors sympathetic to the students were beaten and jailed. The international community of university faculties watched in horror from outside the country as Amin's secret police perpetrated the worst attacks on academic freedom seen anywhere in years. Amin, however, expressed no regrets over their departures or the eventual closure of the country's leading center for higher learning.

Cleansing the Armed Forces

Try as Amin did to solidify the loyalty of the military, some of the most serious threats to his dictatorship came from within its ranks. Following the widespread bloody elimination of Amin's rivals shortly after taking power, anti-Amin opposition sprang up in the barracks. According to Tony Avirgan and Martha Honey, "From the time he seized power until the day he invaded Tanzania [1979], Amin was constantly threatened by dissenting soldiers and preoccupied with how to outmaneuver his opponents within the military."[50]

During 1976 and 1977, sporadic mutinies by individual barracks broke out. On each occasion, Amin countered the mutineers with an overwhelming force of loyal troops. Once the resisters were captured, their punishments were swift and certain. In 1977 an entire barracks of 560 men was arrested and transferred to a prison. During the first week there, they were taken out in small groups and shot. The officers were the first group killed because without them there was no leadership to organize any resistance.

Amin became so paranoid as a result of growing suspicions that he even ordered preemptive attacks on barracks suspected of plotting mutinies. Such acts of ruthless barbarism, unheard of in any other military, were designed to dis-

courage officers and soldiers in other barracks from initiating anti-Amin discussions or plots. Although Amin may have thought that fear would control his army, it had the opposite effect on some officers.

Several officers, even a few high-ranking ones from his own Kakwa tribe, plotted his downfall. Some were arrested and quietly executed without a trial. One particular attempt at a coup, however, caught the attention of all of Kampala. Two high-level officers, one a general and the other a lieutenant colonel, both Christians from Amin's Kakwa tribe, led a commando raid that successfully seized a radio station and Amin's command post in the capital city. However, Amin was not at the post, and by the next morning Amin's soldiers used tanks to kill the mutineers, including the two leaders.

Around this time, Amin's wife, Kay, was accused of being an informant to the mutineers. Her body was later discovered stuffed in the trunk of a car and when it was removed, the medical examiner was horrified to find that it had been dismembered.

Crushing Christian Nonviolent Resistance

While many segments of the Ugandan population were ready to eliminate Amin by violent means if necessary, some, such as the Christian Church, attempted nonviolent strategies. The Christian Church had played a major

Wives of Amin

Although Amin's family life remains cloaked in mystery, he was known to have more than thirty mistresses and an estimated thirty-four children by a variety of women. The story of his wives continues to be a bizarre yet intriguing one. Amin officially recognized five wives, each known to be beautiful, yet each experienced troubled marriages. Of the five, the two wives that captured international interest were his first, Malyamu, and his fourth, Kay Adroa.

Malyamu, the daughter of an educator and sister of Foreign Minister Wanume Kibedi, met Amin when he was a twenty-eight-year-old sergeant in the KAR. She was statuesque at six feet tall, in her early twenties, and was known to enjoy physical activity as did Amin. She was also strong willed, intelligent, and possessed the maturity of a much older woman. Although she had several children with Amin, they did not marry until many years later.

While married to Amin, Malyamu's life took a turn for the worse when her husband met Kay Adroa. Some say Amin had Malyamu's car rammed by his bodyguards to remove her so he could marry Kay. As a result, Malyamu was hospitalized in Mulago Hospital with serious fractures to her arm and leg. While she was recuperating, Amin insulted her on her hospital bed and then had her placed under arrest by his secret police. Seizing an opportunity, she escaped from the hospital and fled to London, where she continues to live working as a waitress. She left her children behind to be raised by Amin's other wives. While Amin was alive, he sent Malyamu a small monthly stipend with the understanding that she was never to make public anything about her life with him.

Amin's marriage to Kay was even more bizarre and tragic. He wanted a beautiful, young wife from his own tribal area, and she fit the profile. She was the daughter of a clergyman, had a college education, and was quiet and dignified. However, Kay was soon found dead, badly mutilated and dismembered. When Amin was notified, he claimed that she had been unfaithful to him and that she had died when her secret lover attempted a surgical abortion on her. Researcher Frederick Guweddeko of Makerere University agrees, contending that the lover dismembered her to create the appearance that Amin had done it. Amin's house servants, however, claim Amin ordered the dismemberment and that he then forced his children to view their mother's body while he shouted at them that their mother had been bad.

role in the lives of many Ugandans for several generations, and Amin feared its power and influence. Amin viewed it as a leftover remnant of British colonialism. To him, championing Ugandan nationalism meant ridding Uganda of all remnants of the British colonial era, and Christianity was one of the last vestiges that had to go. Combined with Amin's opposition to Christianity was a swell of support for Islam moving across all of Africa. For these reasons, Amin promoted the Muslim religion and its mosques at the expense of Christianity and its churches. To protect themselves from the advance of Islam and Amin's attacks, Uganda's Christian churches moved to oppose Amin, and in so doing they became yet another target.

All Christian churches in Uganda suffered terribly under Amin's call for an all-Islamic nation. David Gwyn, who was living in Uganda during Amin's terror, observed that Amin referred to the Catholic Church as "our big enemy which is stopping us from making Uganda Muslim."[51] Following reprisals by Amin loyalists that ranged from burning churches to threatening to kill Catholics who did not convert to Islam, church leaders took action. Intentionally avoiding violent confrontations, the Anglican Church drafted a carefully worded protest letter. It opposed the forceful manner with which the army had invaded churches, killed spiritual leaders, and forced Christians to convert to Islam. The letter also addressed

the growing number of disappearing Ugandans and the alarming number of dead that had been buried in unmarked mass graves. The letter ended with this appeal to stop the violence: "The gun, which was meant to protect Uganda as a nation, the Ugandan as a citizen, and his property is increasingly being used against the Ugandan to take away his life and his property."[52]

The letter was addressed to Amin but copies were also sent to Ugandan religious leaders of all faiths and others living around the world. Amin descended into a dark fury when he read the letter and saw the list of national and international spiritual leaders who had received copies.

This was another moment of international humiliation almost as widely reported as the expulsion of the Asians. On January 16, 1977, Amin called for an official meeting of his diplomats, his cabinet, his senior officials, and the heads of government departments. He also summoned the hierarchy of the Anglican Church. Once assembled, Amin ordered Anglican archbishop Janani Luwum, the highest-ranking Anglican spiritual leader in Uganda, and all of his bishops to stand forward of those assembled. Following a lengthy verbal attack that humiliated and berated them, Archbishop Luwum was placed in a car and driven off. That evening, his dead body was discovered in a wrecked car. Foreign journalists were summoned to photograph the mangled car with

Amin's increasing paranoia meant no one around him was safe.

Luwum's body slumped at the steering wheel as proof of his accidental death. The journalists, however, pointed out to their readers that they had photographed a dead politician in the same crumpled car the previous week.

The archbishop's murder became a turning point in the effective mobilization of the world against Amin. Several of Amin's ministers outside Uganda at the time defected upon hearing the gruesome news, most nations severed diplomatic ties with Amin, and the United Nations held debates on how best to handle him. He was now being referred to by world leaders as a madman and a butcher—and, according to reputable news sources, the British and Israeli governments were even discussing assassinating him.

Silencing Assassins

As foreign opposition discussed assassination attempts, so did organized internal opposition. Kenneth Ingram, in his book *Obote: A Political Biography*, expressed that "there appeared to be a feeling that if all those who were opposed to Amin could organize themselves there was a lively prospect that he might be eliminated."[53] Groups and individuals made attempts to assassinate the man who increasingly displayed signs of madness. By 1977 one African publication tallied twelve known assassination attempts, most of them within the past two years. Other reliable sources suggest the number was much higher.

Amin was well aware that he had become a target. That awareness further destabilized him, and he feared that at any moment a stranger in a crowd or a close friend might assassinate him. Amin was always prepared for assassination attempts. He once confided in Henry Kyemba that he owned an assault rifle that could double as a wire cutter. Amin said, "If they have you

Raid on Entebbe Airport

On June 27, 1976, an Air France airliner bound from Tel Aviv to Paris was hijacked by five members of the Palestine Liberation Organization (PLO), a terrorist group known for their hostility toward Israelis, and two members of the radical German Baader-Meinhof gang. The hijackers forced the plane to land at Entebbe Airport in Uganda, where they demanded the release of fifty-three PLO prisoners held in Israeli prisons in return for the 256 hostages on board the plane, most of whom were Israeli citizens.

Some diplomats believe the hijackers chose Entebbe because Amin was strongly linked to the PLO and might be sympathetic to their demands. Others believe that the hijackers were invited by Amin to come to Entebbe. Once on the ground, Amin offered the hijackers the abandoned Israeli embassy as their headquarters for negotiations with the Israelis.

As Amin became involved in the negotiations for the exchange of the PLO prisoners for the hostages, his sympathies for the hijackers prompted the Israeli government to take action. After one week of little progress, and unbeknownst to Amin, Israeli paratroopers launched Operation Thunderbolt by attacking the airport and freeing almost all the hostages while killing all of the hijackers and twenty Ugandan soldiers attempting to repel their attack. Ten Ugandan fighter jets were destroyed by the paratroopers to prevent them from retaliating against departing Israeli planes.

One Israeli hostage, Dora Bloch, who had been taken to a Kampala hospital, was left behind. After the raid, according to Uganda's minister of health at the time, Henry Kyemba, Mrs. Bloch was taken screaming from her hospital bed and brutally executed the same day by order of Amin.

Amin's refusal to arrest the hijackers and his apparent sympathy for them did much to convince the world that the international community was dealing with a madman. At the end of July, Britain broke off diplomatic relations with Amin's regime.

surrounded, you can cut wires and escape through a fence."[54]

Amin's fear of assassination led to even more suspicious and erratic behavior. Trusting no one and suspecting everyone, Amin began to avoid meetings outside of his office, no longer visited his troops, slept with a loaded automatic rifle at his bedside, and ordered a custom-made, bullet-proof automobile. According to his bodyguards, "Amin darted unpredictably from one heavily guarded residence or hotel to another, frequently changing cars and making few public appearances."[55]

Not knowing who might attack him caused Amin to kill with even greater abandon. To make matters worse, members of the PSU and the SRB were charged with collecting information on potential assassins. They paid informants for information, a reckless tactic that lined their pockets and encouraged false identifications. Those identified were picked up and brought to SRB headquarters for interrogation. Since most, if not all, had been falsely accused, their denials were met with torture until they confessed or died. Compounding the tragedy were those who sought to avoid death by providing names of other innocent people. In such a reign of terror, no one could feel safe.

What Amin could not know was that his days were numbered. He had alienated so many elements of Ugandan society that it was simply a matter of time until someone would kill or expel him.

Chapter Seven

EXILE AND CONDEMNATION

In late 1978 the end was near. Rumors began to circulate that a few of Amin's loyal military units composed of soldiers from his own tribe were on the edge of mutiny. Without the unflinching loyalty of these troops, Amin would be finished. At this point, he understood that his only response was to move decisively against the mutineers with troops whom he hoped were still loyal. Amin was in a serious, if not the most serious, bind of his life.

The Invasian of Tanzania

In October 1978 Amin was on the verge of his own downfall. Military units located on the border shared with Tanzania were threatening mutiny. Amin deployed his mercenaries against the mutineers, some of whom fled across the Tanzanian border.

Amin then falsely claimed that Tanzanian president Nyerere, his perennial enemy, had been at the root of his troubles. At this time, Obote was living there in exile as a guest of Nyerere. Amin accused Nyerere of encouraging the mutiny of the Ugandan troops and of waging war against Uganda. Historians widely agree that Amin was actually hoping to divert attention from his internal troubles and rally Uganda against a foreign adversary.

On November 1, 1978, Amin drove his forces into Tanzanian territory while chasing Ugandan mutineers across the border. He formally annexed a section of territory across the Kagera River boundary. He took this radical act of war because of hostility toward Nyerere, who had been harboring Obote for years and because of suspicions that

Amin fires a rocket launcher while surrounded by loyal troops.

Nyerere was coordinating an invasion of Uganda with Obote. Nyerere responded by mobilizing his army reserves to counterattack, joined by Ugandan exiles united as the Uganda National Liberation Army (UNLA). The armies fought but the Ugandan army retreated steadily, expending much of its energy looting villages along the way. Amin asked Colonel Muammar Qaddafi of Libya for assistance. Qaddafi responded by sending three thousand troops to aid fellow Muslim Amin. However, the Libyans soon found themselves on the frontline, while behind them some of the Ugandan army units were using supply trucks to carry their newly plundered wealth in the opposite direction.

For the next four months, the coalition armies of Obote and Nyerere pushed across the border into Uganda, where they met resistance from fresh units of loyal and well-trained Ugandan troops. The fighting moved from the north in a southward direction through dozens of villages until Amin's forces were driven into Kampala, where they would make their final stand. The invading army encircled the nation's capital, cut off electricity, fuel, and clean water, and offered amnesty to all Ugandan fighters if they would surrender.

On April 11, 1979, Tanzania and the UNLA entered Kampala against little resistance. Nyerere allowed Obote to return with the victorious army and Obote installed himself as president of Uganda. Seeing that the end was

Foreign-Planned Assassinations

By 1977 foreign governments expressed the need to eliminate the reckless dictator. The two willing to do so openly were Britain and Israel. Both countries had generated a strong antipathy toward Amin.

British foreign secretary Lord Owen, speaking on the radio shortly following Amin's death, admitted that he had recommended assassinating Amin. Although some apparently saw his proposal as an outrageous suggestion, Owen confided in the article "UK Considered Killing Idi Amin," found on the BBC World News Web site: "I'm not ashamed of considering it, because his regime goes down in the scale of Pol Pot [murderous Cambodian dictator] as one of the worst of all recent regimes."

Lord Owen was not the lone influential Briton proposing an assassination. Harold Wilson, prime minister during the mid-1970s, also wanted Amin dead. At the time, it was being reported to Wilson that Amin was killing seven thousand people a week. In the same BBC interview, the press secretary to the prime minister, Joe Hines, revealed:

Harold called me up to his study and said that he was very concerned about this. He asked me my view about killing Idi Amin, as he thought that was the only way of stopping the slaughter. I was against capital punishment, but I said that in this case we should make an exception. He was very concerned about Africa, and Amin, and he told me he was going to take the idea up with the Foreign Office. Amin was a madman indulging in the mass slaughter of his people.

Officials in the British government failed to act because the British government did not have agents trained to carry out such a mission.

Israel expressed an interest in assassinating Amin, recommending that the man who led the raid on Entebbe Airport, Colonel Bolka Bar-Lev, take command. With financial support from Ugandan refugees, Bar-Lev agreed to a fee of $1.5 million in exchange for killing Amin and his top officers. The assassination attempt, however, never took place.

inevitable, Qaddafi sent aircraft to rescue the remainder of his Libyan troops as well as one plane to carry Amin and his immediate family to safety in Libya.

With Amin out and Obote in, the same crowds that had danced in the street in 1971 were dancing once again in 1979. Eluding capture with his flight to Libya, Amin left behind an impoverished Uganda and a brutalized people. During his eight years of rule, he had instituted no domestic or foreign policies yet had managed to expel all Asians, kill three hundred thousand Ugandans, spend excessively to build up his army, and drive the economy of the Pearl of Africa into the ground. As George Ivan Smith wrote: "Amin came to power on the basis of empty promises to them all. None was fulfilled and no sectors of the population apart from his own Nubians and Muslims derived any benefit from the society created by his army axis."[56]

In Search of a New Home

Qaddafi welcomed Amin to Libya for three reasons: their long-standing friendship, support of the Muslim religion, and shared amimosity toward the Israelis. To accommodate Amin's exile, Qaddafi provided Amin with one of his villas on the Tripoli coast of the Mediterranean where Amin talked of an immediate return to Uganda to expel the Tanzanian invaders and punish the Ugandan rebels.

Within a few months of his arrival, however, the friendship between the two men became strained. Amin insisted that his bodyguards stay with him at all times, while Qaddafi, who distrusted them, argued that Libyan security forces were better able to provide the protection Amin demanded. Recognizing that he may not have found the best country for his exile, Amin accepted an invitation from President Saddam Hussein to relocate to Iraq.

Amin arrived in Baghdad, the capital of Iraq, just months after Hussein took formal control as its president. Hussein proclaimed Iraq to be a new Islamic republic and, like Qaddafi and Amin, he was an avid opponent of the Israelis. But Amin realized that he had exercised poor judgment in deciding to live in Baghdad under the newly constituted regime of Hussein.

While in Baghdad, Amin witnessed Hussein dispense the same sort of terror that he himself had unleashed in Kampala. To solidify his power, Hussein began a period of purging and consolidation that cost many their lives and drove thousands of Shiite Muslims of Iranian origin back to Iran. Lost in the confusion of revolution and not wishing to be caught in potential violence, Amin sought exile in a more stable Muslim country and received an invitation from King Faisal of Saudi Arabia.

Exiled to Saudi Arabia

Amin eagerly accepted the offer for sanctuary by the Saudi royal family headed by King Faisal. The reason they gave for accepting a pariah such as Amin

The exiled Amin relaxes at his home in Saudi Arabia.

was that he was a Muslim and that the Muslim holy book, the Koran, required Muslims living in the desert to provide hospitality to other wandering Muslims in need of assistance. Besides, Amin's hatred of Israel endeared him to his hosts.

Amin arrived in Saudi Arabia and was given a villa in the port city of Jeddah on condition that he remain out of politics and not talk to the media while exiled in the country. The Saudis' desire to silence him was motivated by their opinion that Amin's ruthless tyranny had been an embarrassment to Islam, which the Saudi government wished to promote as being a religion of peace and friendship. In the subsequent twenty-four years, he gave very few interviews and stayed close to home. His villa was in an exclusive area occupied by powerful oil sheikhs. All house expenses, including domestic servants and bodyguards, were paid by the Saudi government, in addition to a $1,500 monthly stipend.

Amin's life in Saudi Arabia appears to have revolved around a routine of attending sports events, gym sessions, and massage parlors, and from time to time he played the accordion, fished, swam, and recited from the Koran. He enjoyed driving around parts of Jeddah in a Range Rover, a Chevrolet Caprice, and a powder-blue Cadillac for his shopping trips. He also visited the airport to clear through customs boxes of Ugandan foods, such as cassava flour, fresh cassava, millet flour, and *matoke,* or green bananas, sent by relatives.

While Amin resided in luxury in Jeddah, a few calls for some sort of international justice arose, primarily outside of Uganda. A handful of governments, human rights organizations, and agencies within the United Nations hoped to hold Amin accountable in some sort of international court for his years of murderous rule. Precedent for such a court or international tribunal existed when the Nuremberg trials convened at the end of World War II to try, convict, and execute high-level members of the German government and army. To the disappointment of many, however, the Saudi government refused to extradite Amin for trial.

Shrugging off attempts to try him, Amin longed to return to Uganda. In 1985 an opportunity to return arose when Obote was once again deposed and this time exiled to Zambia. In 1986 Yoweri Museveni became president of Uganda and hoped to create a stable government composed of representatives of all tribal groups. He extended personal invitations to exiled Ugandans, and to many he even offered key government advisory or corporate positions. Museveni was hopeful that these individuals would return and help rebuild a fragmented and broken country.

Amin, along with family members, approached Museveni hoping to negotiate his return. Although Amin occasionally commented that he hoped to return to power, his fifth wife, Nalongo Madina Amin, and their children more modestly asked that Museveni allow Amin to return and live a simple life away from the politics of Kampala. Museveni, however, sensing that Amin might become a liability, denied the request.

Although it violated Amin's agreement with Saudi Arabia not to talk to the media, one rare interview with Amin did take place in 1999. At that time, British Broadcasting Corporation reporter Brian Barron contacted Amin, whom he had previously interviewed in Uganda, and was granted access to Amin's villa to conduct an interview in the presence of his bodyguards. Amin welcomed Barron into the lounge of his villa, where he was playing Scottish bagpipe music. In the course of the forty-five-minute interview, Barron reported:

Historical Difficulties Assessing Amin's Regime

Few modern historical figures have confounded historians as has Amin. Little sound historical information about the dictator is available to historians, who are accustomed to poring over thousands and sometimes millions of records documenting a ruler's reign and personal life. They point to several reasons so little is known about a leader who died so recently. These include his secretive dictatorship and Uganda's minor role in international politics. The one that is most unusual for modern historians is the lack of documentation due to Amin's illiteracy.

Men who counseled Amin often cited his inability to read and write as a major obstacle to his rule. Amin was known to issue legal, political, military, and economic laws and policies by verbal proclamation, unlike most political leaders, who publish formal documents. Amin often relayed orders and policy decisions by telephone to just one person or in long rambling speeches to civil servants who rarely paid close attention. Without written documents, those who did not hear his proclamations were never certain of what he actually said. Historians who are now attempting to reconstruct the details of his rule are at a serious disadvantage because those who heard his announcements often disagree about the details.

Compounding the problem was Amin's disinterest in preserving what little documentation his advisers provided. According to several of his ministers, important files were lost during their transfer by wheelbarrow. The situation became so egregious that many historians consider his government inferior to that of Uganda's precolonial days.

[Amin] was relaxed and clearly homesick, promising he would regain control in Uganda. He rejected any responsibility for the years of brutality, for the murder of his opponents, for the scenes of horror we had witnessed at the SRB headquarters. All had been fabricated by his enemies, he insisted.[57]

Within four years of this last interview, Amin was rushed to King Faisal Hospital, unable to walk, with severe swelling of his extremities, and in a state of semiconsciousness. Amin was placed in an intensive care unit where his prognosis was pronounced to be grim.

Death and Condemnation

On August 16, 2003, following a month-long coma, Amin finally succumbed to high blood pressure and multiple organ failure. The once powerfully built boxing champion had ballooned to four hundred pounds at the end of his life.

Nalongo Madina Amin said that she and two of Amin's sons were with him at the Saudi hospital when he died. She told the newspaper the *Sunday Monitor* that she had approached Ugandan president Museveni some time earlier and asked that Amin be allowed to return to Uganda to die but was told the former dictator would have to "answer for his sins."[58]

Edith Ssempala, Ugandan ambassador to the United States, denied charges that the Ugandan government had denied a family request to bury the dictator in Uganda. "He could have been buried in Uganda. It's just when Muslims die, they are buried immediately. There's just no way he could have been brought to Uganda in time."[59] Commenting on news of Idi Amin's death, Uganda's presidential spokesman ex-

A Ugandan newspaper vendor hawks the news of Amin's death in 2003.

pressed satisfaction, calling his death "good"—a sentiment shared by many.

As news of Amin's death spread around the globe, many who knew him spoke out condemning his brutal tyranny that cost hundreds of thousands their lives. Yasmin Alibhai-Brown, a Ugandan Asian newspaper columnist whose family was among those Amin expelled, said the Saudis should have brought him to justice:

> I think it is a disgrace that Saudi Arabia gave him the kind of life they did, and the excuse is he was a Muslim. They should have delivered him into the hands of international justice, and they never did. And for the families of all those victims, black African families, this is going to be something they'll never forgive.[60]

Ambassador Ssempala said history would remember Amin

> as he should be remembered: a brutal, vicious, dictatorial leader of Uganda. I don't think he has ever shown any remorse. He has even been proud of that. He knew he was killing people. He seemed even to be enjoying it. He killed even his own wife. This is something that quite frankly is difficult to understand, that a human being can have no heart.[61]

Despite Amin's well-documented crimes against humanity, he escaped prosecution because the Saudi authorities shielded him from those who sought to bring him to justice. Nonetheless, while ensconced in his villa in Jeddah and after his death, an international outcry reaching far beyond Uganda and Saudi Arabia swept the globe.

International Outcry

Condemnation of Amin was not confined to Africa and the Middle East. Following two decades of comfortable exile in Saudi Arabia, many government and civic leaders throughout the international community expressed their outrage. How could it be possible, they asked, for a known sadistic mass murderer to live a protected life shielded from a trial for his crimes? Such a question, lacking a reasonable answer, underscored the need for a system that could bring tyrants to justice for crimes against humanity.

George Ngwa, a spokesman for Amnesty International, an international organization dedicated to protecting human rights, said in a statement following the tyrant's death:

> Amin's death is a sad comment on the international community's inability to hold leaders accountable for gross human rights abuses. The fact that Idi Amin was able to evade justice for over two decades underlines the present need for an international justice system that can hold people responsible for genocide, crimes against humanity, and other grave human rights abuses.[62]

Ambassador Moynihan at the United Nations

The United Nations and other world organizations were periodically subjected to scathing denunciations by governments for failing to rein in Amin and hold him accountable for his brutal acts that cost the lives of many Ugandans. Although it is true that the United Nations failed to intervene on behalf of Ugandans, some within the organization spoke out against Amin and his atrocious behavior.

In 1975 a scathing denouncement of the United Nations vis-à-vis Amin was delivered by American ambassador to the United Nations, Daniel Patrick Moynihan. In his speech, Moynihan referred to Amin as a racist murderer. Although diplomats were horrified that Moynihan would make such a blatantly offensive comment, supporters of Moynihan were quick to point out that they ought to have been far more horrified by Amin's murderous actions.

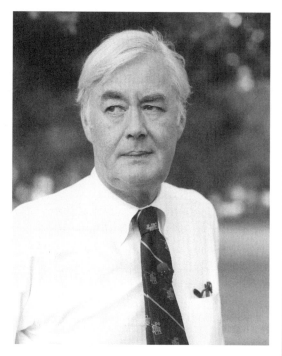

In 1975 U.S. ambassador to the United Nations Daniel Patrick Moynihan denounced Amin as a racist murderer and berated fellow diplomats for allowing Amin's atrocities.

Moynihan then railed at his fellow diplomats for turning their backs on Ugandans and for not caring enough about them to suppress Amin. Because of Moynihan's attack on Amin and diplomats who would not confront the "Butcher of Uganda"—as he was regularly called by the press—many people labeled the United Nations as being a morally bankrupt institution.

Because of the impact that Moynihan's confrontation had with his colleagues at the United Nations, other dictators following Amin received tougher treatment. Since the late 1970s, the United Nations has committed troops to war-torn, beleaguered nations and has arrested and placed derelict leaders on trial for crimes against humanity.

Many criticized Ugandan president Yoweri Museveni's government for failing to bring Amin to justice before he lay on his deathbed. James Tumusiime, a writer for the Ugandan newspaper the *Monitor*, commented, "If the . . . government felt so strongly against Amin's atrocities, how come there was no attempt to extradite him from Saudi Arabia?"[63]

Another human rights group, the New York–based Human Rights Watch, added their critical voice to the international outrage. Reed Brody, director of special prosecutions, joined other rights organizations in his criticism of the lack of prosecution by saying:

> We regret that Idi Amin is dying without meeting justice for his crimes. Amin was one of the bloodiest tyrants in a bloody century. It's increasingly possible to prosecute dictators outside their home countries. Unfortunately, the trend didn't catch up with Mr. Amin in time.[64]

Many people have wondered why the United Nations did not step in. According to representatives of the United Nations, it had not set up the International Criminal Court to deal with cases of genocide and crimes against humanity until July 2002. The future, however, looks more promising. Brody says he sees a new international determination to get tough on dictators:

> There has been a fundamental shift in the way the world deals with perpetrators of atrocities. We used to say that if you killed one person, you went to jail. If you killed 10 people, you were put in an insane asylum. And if you killed 10,000 people, you got invited to a peace conference.[65]

Brody later added: "It's too bad that death caught up with Idi Amin before justice did. Amin was responsible for widespread murder and the expulsion of his country's Asian community, and yet he was able to escape reckoning."[66]

NOTES

Introduction: One Frog Spoils a Waterhole

1. Quoted in *African History*, "Idi Amin Dada," 2003. www.african history.about.com.
2. Dr. Sunny Orumen Akhigbe, "A Dinosaur Reduced to an Ant," *Africa News Service*, November 24, 2003, section B, page 3.
3. Henry Kyemba, *A State of Blood: The Inside Story of Idi Amin*. New York: Ace Books, 1977, p. 24.
4. Quoted in David Lamb, "Idi Amin, Tyrant of Uganda, Is Dead," *The Age*, August 17, 2003. www.theage.com.au.
5. Thomas and Margaret Melady, *Idi Amin Dada: Hitler in Africa*. Kansas City: Sheed Andrews and McMeel, 1977, p. 181.
6. Kenneth Ingram, *Obote: A Political Biography*. London: Routledge, 1994, p. 23.
7. David Gwyn, *Idi Amin: Death-Light of Africa*. Boston: Little, Brown, 1977, p. 3.

Chapter 1: Early Influences

8. David Martin, *General Amin*. London: Faber, 1974, p. 14.

9. Quoted in *BBC World News*, "Imperial Racism," May 2003. www.bbc.co.uk.

Chapter 2: From Cook to Chief of Staff

10. Quoted in George Ivan Smith, *Ghosts of Kampala: The Rise and Fall of Idi Amin*. New York: St. Martin's, 1980, p. 50.
11. Smith, *Ghosts of Kampala*, p. 48.
12. Quoted in Smith, *Ghosts of Kampala*, p. 26.
13. Quoted in Martin, *General Amin*, p. 20.
14. Quoted in Smith, *Ghosts of Kampala*, p. 52.
15. Kyemba, *A State of Blood*, p. 25.
16. Ingram, *Obote*, p. 89.
17. Kyemba, *A State of Blood*, p. 27.

Chapter 3: Building a Base of Political Support

18. Quoted in "Idi Amin Dada Oumee," *Moreorless*, 2003. www.moreorless.com.au.
19. Smith, *Ghosts of Kampala*, p. 63.
20. Quoted in Smith, *Ghosts of Kampala*, p. 68.
21. Quoted in Linda de Hoyos, "Idi Amin: London Stooge Against

Sudan," *Executive Intelligence Review,* June 9, 1995, p. 52.

22. Quoted in Smith, *Ghosts of Kampala,* p. 66.
23. Kyemba, *A State of Blood,* p. 32.
24. Kyemba, *A State of Blood,* p. 32.
25. Smith, *Ghosts of Kampala,* p. 53.
26. Smith, *Ghosts of Kampala,* p. 78.
27. Gwyn, *Idi Amin,* pp. 54–55.
28. Martin, *General Amin,* p. 26.

Chapter 4: Emergence of the Tyrant

29. Quoted in Martin, *General Amin,* p. 27.
30. Quoted in Martin, *General Amin,* pp. 27–28.
31. Quoted in Martin, *General Amin,* p. 23.
32. Gwyn, *Idi Amin,* p. 161.
33. Martin, *General Amin,* p. 131.
34. Martin, *General Amin,* p. 133.
35. Tony Avirgan and Martha Honey, *War in Uganda: The Legacy of Idi Amin.* Westport, CT: Lawrence Hill, 1982, p. 31.
36. Kyemba, *A State of Blood,* p. 112.

Chapter 5: Expulsion of the Asians

37. Smith, *Ghosts of Kampala,* p. 97.
38. Quoted in "If Only the Queen Had Asked Him to Tea," *The Daily Telegraph,* August 2, 2002. www.ismaili.net/timeline/2002/20020802dt.html.
39. Quoted in "If Only the Queen Had Asked Him to Tea."

40. Martin, *General Amin,* p. 168.
41. Smith, *Ghosts of Kampala,* p. 98.
42. Quoted in Avirgan and Honey, *War in Uganda,* p. 4.
43. Kyemba, *A State of Blood,* p. 240.
44. Quoted in Martin, *General Amin,* p. 165.
45. Kyemba, *A State of Blood,* p. 139.
46. Martin, *General Amin,* p. 140.

Chapter Six: Rooting Out Internal Opposition

47. Quoted in Avirgan and Honey, *War in Uganda,* p. 28.
48. Gwyn, *Idi Amin,* p. 181.
49. Quoted in Smith, *Ghosts of Kampala,* p. 147.
50. Avirgan and Honey, *War in Uganda,* p. 30.
51. Quoted in Gwyn, *Idi Amin,* p. 112.
52. Quoted in Smith, *Ghosts of Kampala,* p. 151.
53. Ingram, *Obote,* p. 144
54. Kyemba, *A State of Blood,* p. 141.
55. Quoted in Avirgan and Honey, *War in Uganda,* p. 51.

Chapter 7: Exile and Condemnation

56. Smith, *Ghosts of Kampala,* p. 30.
57. Brian Barron, "The Idi Amin I Knew," BBC News, August 16, 2003. http://news.bbc.co.uk.
58. BBC News, "Idi Amin Back in Media Spotlight," July 25, 2003. http://news.bbc.co.uk
59. Quoted in "No Going Home for Amin: Ugandan Dictator Idi

Amin Buried in Saudi Arabia," *BiafraNigeriaWorld News*, August 17, 2003. www.news.biafranigeria world.com.

60. Yasmin Alibhai-Brown, "Former Ugandan Dictator Idi Amin Dies," *CNN.com*, August 16, 2003. www.cnn.com.

61. Quoted in Alibhai-Brown "Former Ugandan Dictator Idi Amin Dies."

62. Quoted in "Amin's Death Shows Failure of International System: Amnesty," *Sydney Morning Herald*, August 17, 2003. www.smh.com.au.

63. James Tumusiime, "Dead Amin is Useless to Museveni's Mov't," *Monitor*, July 29, 2003. www.monitor.co.ug.

64. Reed Brody, "Amin Should Have Faced Justice," *Human Rights Watch*, July 22, 2003. www.hrw.org.

65. Quoted in Mark Baker, "Justice Is Fickle When It Comes to Former Dictators," *Truth News,* 2003. www.truthnews.net.

66. Reed Brody, "Uganda: Idi Amin Dies Without Facing Justice," *Human Rights Watch*, August 18, 2003. www.hrw.org/press/2003/ 08/uganda081803.htm.

FOR FURTHER READING

Books

Sir Peter Allen, *Interesting Times: Life in Uganda Under Idi Amin*. New York: Trans-Atlantic Publications, 2000. Peter Allen spent over thirty years in Uganda, first as a policeman, then as a law lecturer. Allen's diaries as a policeman under the Idi Amin government record his efforts to find some order and discipline from the chaos enveloping him.

Martin Jamison, *Idi Amin and Uganda: An Annotated Bibliography*. New York: Greenwood Publishing, 1992. This book provides a collection of published material on Idi Amin and Uganda during his rule. Entries are arranged topically within chronological sections and cover the span of Amin's reign from 1971 to 1979.

Thomas Melady, *Uganda: The Asian Exiles*. New York: Orbis Books, 1976. Melady, who was the British ambassador to Uganda for two years while Amin was in power, provides a detailed discussion on the expulsion of the Asians and describes the collapse of the Ugandan economy following their departure.

Web Sites

Africana (www.africana.com). This site focuses on stories about Africa, including history, contemporary events, cultural offerings, current politics, sports, and fashion.

BBC News (www.news.bbc.co.uk). This site, provided by the British Broadcasting Company, provides one of the most respected news Web sites in the world. It is filled daily with hundreds of news stories from around the world.

Human Rights Watch (www.hrw.org). Human Rights Watch is a nonprofit organization dedicated to protecting the human rights of people around the world. The Web site provides articles about human rights violations and information about how they can be stopped.

Works Consulted

Books

Tony Avirgan and Martha Honey. *War in Uganda: The Legacy of Idi Amin*. Westport, CT: Lawrence Hill, 1982. Highlights Uganda's economic collapse beginning with the departure of the British and culminating with the expulsion of the Asian merchant class. The book adds insight into Amin's cruelty and cunning manipulation of Ugandan political factions.

David Gwyn, *Idi Amin: Death-Light of Africa*. Boston: Little, Brown, 1977. David Gwyn, a Ugandan who worked for Amin before fleeing to England, provides an excellent history of Amin and his oppressive tyrannical rule. The book contains many eyewitness accounts of Amin's actions, his secret police, and his oppressive rule in Kampala.

Kenneth Ingram, *Obote: A Political Biography*. London: Routledge, 1994. Ingram's book is a biography of Obote; however, it provides considerable detail about Amin's regime as it intersects with Obote's fall from power and his subsequent return.

Henry Kyemba, *A State of Blood: The Inside Story of Idi Amin*. New York: Ace Books, 1977. Kyemba spent five years as Amin's minister of health and knew him well. His book reflects his intimate knowledge of Amin, detailing the atrocities and the day-to-day life of Amin. The book includes an interesting collection of black-and-white photographs.

Mahmood Mamdani, *Imperialism and Fascism in Uganda*. Nairobi: Heinemann Educational Books, 1983. Mamdani analyzes the violent complexities of Amin's politics, and he attempts to explain the reasons Amin was able to survive in power as long as he did.

David Martin, *General Amin*. London: Faber, 1974. This book traces Amin's rise to power and his rule through 1973. Martin provides more detail than most accounts, including horrifying descriptions of brutal beatings and murders.

Thomas and Margaret Melady, *Idi Amin Dada: Hitler in Africa*. Kansas City: Sheed Andrews and McMeel, 1977. Thomas Melady was the

British ambassador to Uganda from 1972 to 1974. In this book he and his wife reveal first-hand experiences of living in Uganda during Amin's rule.

George Ivan Smith, *Ghosts of Kampala: The Rise and Fall of Idi Amin*. New York: St. Martin's, 1980. Smith, a United Nations official during the 1970s, drew upon his experiences to form a good portrait of Amin. He starts with an informative discussion of Amin's youth and career followed by his presidency of Uganda.

Periodicals

Dr. Sunny Orumen Akhigbe, "A Dinosaur Reduced to an Ant," *Africa News Service*, November 24, 2003.

Linda de Hoyos, "Idi Amin: London Stooge Against Sudan," *Executive Intelligence Review*, June 9, 1995.

Internet Sources

African History, "Idi Amin Dada," 2003. www.africanhistory.about.com.

Mark Baker, "Justice Is Fickle When It Comes to Former Dictators," *Truth News*, 2003. www.truthnews.net.

Brian Barron, "Death of a Despot," Islam online, www.islamonline.net.

———, "The Idi Amin I Knew," BBC News, August 16, 2003. http://news.bbc.co.uk.

BBC News, "Dictator Idi Amin Dies," August 17, 2003. http://news.bbc.co.uk.

———, "Idi Amin Back in Media Spotlight," July 25, 2003. http://news.bbc.co.uk.

———, "Idi Amin in Quotes," August 16, 2003. http://news. bbc.co.uk.

BBC World News, "Imperial Racism," May 2003. www.bbc.co.uk.

———, "UK Considered Killing Idi Amin," August 2003. www.bbc.co.uk.

BiafraNigeria World News, "No Going Home for Amin: Ugandan Dictator Idi Amin Buried in Saudi Arabia," August 17, 2003. www.news.biafra nigeriaworld.com.

Reed Brody, "Amin Should Have Faced Justice," *Human Rights Watch*, July 22, 2003. www.hrw.org.

———, "Idi Amin at Death's Door: Despots Should Not Rest in Peace," *Human Rights Watch*, July 25, 2003. www.hrw.org.

———, "Uganda: Idi Amin Dies Without Facing Justice," *Human Rights Watch*, August 18, 2003. www.hrw.org.

CNN.com, "Former Ugandan Dictator Idi Amin dies," August 16, 2003. www.cnn.com.

Bob Congress, "The Words of the Honorable Field Marshal General Idi Amin Dada," Bob Congress. www. bobocongress.com.

The Daily Telegraph, If Only the Queen Had Asked Him to Tea," August 2, 2002. www. ismaili.net/timeline/2002/20020802dt.html

Richard Dowden, "Why Israel and Britain Were Delighted at Amin's Rise," MShale.com. www.mshale.com.

Geocities, "A Clown Drenched in Brutality," August 17, 2003. www.geocities.com.

Denis Hills, "Idi Amin Dada Oumee," Moreorless, 2003. www.moreorless.au.com.

E.B. Idowu, "Idi Amin, the Little-Big Man: Thoughts on His Life and Death, *Out of Africa*, 2003. www.kabiza.com.

Kigezi International School of Medicine, "The Pearl of Africa," 2003. www. kigezi.edu.

David Lamb, "Idi Amin, Tyrant of Uganda, Is Dead," *The Age*, August 17, 2003. www.theage.com.au.

Steven Niven, "Idi Amin: Crazy Like a Fascist," *Africana*, August 18, 2003. www.africana.com.

Sydney Morning Herald, "Amin's Death Shows Failure of International System: Amnesty," August 17, 2003. www.smh.com.au.

James Tumusiime, "Dead Amin Is Useless to Museveni's Mov't," *Monitor*, July 29, 2003. www.monitor. co.ug.

Index

PICTURE CREDITS

About the Author

James Barter received his undergraduate degree in history and classics at the University of California, Berkeley, followed by graduate studies in ancient history and archaeology at the University of Pennsylvania. Mr. Barter has taught history as well as Latin and Greek.

A Fulbright scholar at the American Academy in Rome, Mr. Barter worked on archaeological sites in and around the city as well as on sites in the Naples area. He also has worked and traveled extensively in Greece.

Mr. Barter currently resides in Rancho Santa Fe, California.